AF520336

Education
Reform Strategy

Dear Authors

Our message to the world is that India can win the battle not only by the bullet but also by the pen. There is no dearth of intellectuals in our country, but their knowledge is confined to them only. No sincere effort has been made by any other publisher to channelise their knowledge in national interest. That is why the talent of a large number of intellectuals remains latent. An author transforms his knowledge into a manuscript, and it is our job to spread his/her knowledge by converting it into a beautiful book. We are constantly motivating the intellectuals for writing/ publishing their manuscripts and would like to publish your manuscript too. If you or your colleagues have any manuscript ready for publication or are working on it, kindly contact us with detailed synopsis and list of contents. We will transform your work into a valuable publication. If you wish, we can also suggest you the suitable subjects for writing the books related to your area of expertise. We are known for its publishing quality and commitments. We take utmost care in production and give wide publicity to the book as well as its author through our national and international distribution network.

Education Reform Strategy

United Nations Relief and Work Agency (UNRWA)

Books for Libraries

Delhi-110042

Books for Libraries
B-420, Shahbad Daulatpur,
Near Vikram Dharam Kanta
Delhi-110042
Ph: 9868224781
E-mail: booksforlibraries@hotmail.com

United Nations Relief and Work Agency (UNRWA)

2017

ISBN : 978-81-926482-7-9

₹ 495/-

The complete text/data etc have been written and provided by the author only. The publisher is not responsible for the views of the author and authenticity of the data, in any manner whatsoever.

All disputes are subject to Delhi Jurisdiction only. No other court will have the Jurisdiction to entertain any case except the competent court of Delhi.

Printed in India at
R.K. Print Service, Delhi
and published by Mrs Rekha Garg for
Books For Libraries,
B-420, Shahbad Daulatpur,
Near Vikram Dharam Kanta,
New Delhi-110042 (INDIA)

Contents

Annexes

Acknowledgements

This report was produced by the Director of Education, Dr Caroline Pontefract. It reflects the inputs and discussions of the UNRWA five Fields of operations from three Reform Strategy Workshops. The Workshops involved key stakeholders from all the Fields, including Deputy Directors, Chiefs of Education, Heads of EDCs, Deans of ESFs and other representatives from Field and Area level, as well as those from Human Resources and PCSU, HQ (Amman).

Executive Summary

1.0 In developing the Education Reform Strategy, UNRWA recognises the need to consider the nature of its external operating context and the developments occurring therein. The organisation will not be unaffected by the broad political, social and economic landscapes of the countries within which it operates. Similarly, the Reform Strategy will be strengthened by an understanding of the educational priorities emerging across the region and within each host country.

2.0 UNRWA's operating context is varied, ranging from the relative stability of Jordan and Syria, where the Palestine refugees enjoy a wide range of rights and opportunities, to the progressively more complex environments of Lebanon, the West Bank and Gaza. Lebanon, effectively a post-conflict environment, presents an ongoing challenge to the Palestine refugees, who are economically and socially marginalized. The ongoing Israeli occupation and a regime of blockage and movement restrictions in the West Bank and Gaza drastically affect the well-being of Palestine refugees.

3.0 The entire region is characterised by growth in youth population, which will lead to significant demographic changes over the coming years, and a consequent increased demand for services, including education. Across the region, the Human Development Index (HDI) performance of UNRWA host countries varies. Lebanon's impressive score places it in the `high human development' category and Jordan's performance is also good when compared with other lower middle-income countries. Syria is urbanising rapidly, and scores just above the occupied Palestinian territory (oPt) which remains acutely affected by poverty.

4.0 UNRWA's operating contexts are experiencing increasingly severe youth unemployment, combined with the challenge of adapting their markets to be competitive in a global economy that is becoming progressively more knowledge-based. The region has been affected by the global financial crisis in differing measures, ranging from reduced remittances from diaspora Palestinians, to large numbers of returning workers, to reduced donor aidflows. Conversely, there have also been some positive effects, particularly in Lebanon, which has benefited from post-global crisis regional portfolio shifts and its reputation as a relatively safe investment destination. In addition to the global financial crisis, the Iraqi refugee crisis has also had a significant socio-economic impact on the region, with Syria, Jordan and Lebanon hosting large numbers of Iraqi refugees since 2003.

5.0 Any educational developments and prioritisation in the region must be situated within the global frameworks of the Millennium Development Goals (MDGs) and the Education For All (EFA) initiative. The principal challenge for the region as a whole, which has made significant progress in enabling children to access school, is to improve quality. UNRWA's host countries are adopting a multifaceted approach to this challenge, namely through investing in Teacher education, Technical and Vocational Education and Training (TVET), Inclusive Education and Information Communication Technology (ICT) as a learning tool to support both students and their teachers.

6.0 Teacher education initiatives in the host countries are focusing on facilitating a pedagogical shift that will enable active learning methodologies to replace more traditional rote-learning approaches. Teacher motivation, retention and continuing professional development is also prioritised, particularly in the oPt, where, for the first time in the region, teacher categories, determined by level of professional experience, are being introduced.

7.0 TVET initiatives across the region are looking to the greater provision of skills training that is relevant to the labour market and increasing links between employers and education and training institutions.

Training in entrepreneurship is also being developed, and flexible routes between TVET and academic training are increasingly encouraged. Strategic use of ICT in schools and ICT capacity building amongst teachers is improving across the region, with Jordan in particular gaining a reputation as a sector leader in this area.

8.0 Initial steps are also being taken across the region to improve Inclusive Education and provision for children with Special Educational Needs (SEN). Although all UNRWA host countries have much progress still to make in this area, growing recognition of the importance of Inclusive Education means that implementation of such programmes is likely to increase over the coming years.

9.0 Alongside the priorities emerging in the national education systems across the region, sit the priorities of the `Non Governmental Organisations' (NGOs) in their education programmes. These priorities range from those linked to the increasing awareness of the value of education in emergencies (relevant to Gaza and the West Bank), to the more widely applicable priorities of skills training and the role of education as related to work, child protection, quality, gender and inclusive education.

10.0 Education work across the region is also affected, and to some extent determined by, major global donors, who are in turn impacted by the financial crisis. It is estimated that an additional 90 million people will have been pushed into poverty in

2011 as a result of the crisis, and inevitably, it is the most vulnerable who will suffer the most. It is essential that education remains a priority for donors, and that UNRWA is adequately equipped to provide services for the children in its care, many of whom are some of the most disadvantaged in the region.

11.0 UNRWA education programme thus operates within this global, regional, and national context. It has provided education for Palestine refugees for over 60 years and this education has been recognised as being equal to, if not better, than that of host countries. The partnership between UNESCO and UNRWA enabled UNRWA to spearhead many quality educational practices across the region. For example in the 1960s, through the use of distance learning, the percentage of UNRWA untrained teachers dropped from 90% to 9%.

12.0 Although proud of the strengths and achievements of the UNRWA education system there has been a growing recognition within, and beyond the Agency, of the need for Reform. This is in line with the overall Reform agenda of the Agency as a whole and, with regard to education, reflects perceptions of declining quality, the results of Agency wide Monitoring Learning Achievements (MLA) tests and the evolving demands of an education system for the 21st century.

13.0 Following the UNRWA Organisational Development (OD) process, which addressed the enabling environment of the Agency—Human Resources, Administration, Finances—evaluations and reviews of the programmes were commissioned. To this effect a comprehensive Review of the UNRWA education programme was undertaken by an external organisation, Universalia. This was completed in February 2010 and provided the foundation for dialogue and decision making in the development of the UNRWA Education Reform Strategy. The Universalia review, its findings and recommendations, is the focus of Chapter 3 and is referred to throughout this Strategy.

14.0 More recently the Agency has embarked on the development of a `Sustaining Change' strategy to give coherence to this second phase of UNRWA reform, a reform which will consolidate and build upon the achievements of the initial phase and will focus specifically on the reform of UNRWA programmatic areas, of which education is one.

15.0 The UNRWA education Reform must therefore be aligned to, and placed within, UNRWA's strategic frameworks. These are most specifically the Medium Term Strategy (MTS), a six year framework from January 2010, the decentralisation process as reflected in the Organisational Development Plan (ODP) of 2006. The ODP describes the relative roles and responsibilities of Headquarters and Fields, but there is a need to clarify this through the implementation of the Reform. Lessons learned through the decentralised planning processes—HIP and FIPs—will also be reflected in future Agency wide planning processes and this will support greater coherence.

16.0 Between February and September, 2010 the Education Department led a process to develop an Agency wide Education Reform Strategy. A number of workshops and retreats took place to identify, prepare and develop a Reform Strategy, one which would serve to enhance the effectiveness, efficiency, and quality of education provision for the 500,000 Palestine refugees students enrolled in the 691 schools, 10 VTCs and three Education Science Faculties across the five Fields of UNRWA's operation.

17.0 At the heart of the Reform Strategy is the classroom and the teaching and learning pedagogy, that is the way in which teachers interact with their students. To change the ethos of the schools and their classrooms will require establishing an enabling, supportive environment at all levels. As educational experience indicates, and the Universalia Review emphasises, quality education is unlikely to be achieved through focusing on single strands or dimensions of education practices, such as teacher training alone.

18.0 Transformational change towards enhanced quality education in UNRWA will therefore depend upon a holistic, coherent and interrelated approach. To this effect the Education Reform draws upon the analysis of the whole UNRWA education system in order to determine action to be taken to improve overall quality. The Reform Strategy thus comprises eight (8) key dimensions, all of which interact and interrelate with each other. For example, to enhance teacher performance teachers undoubtedly need to be effectively trained, but they also need to be well-selected, professionally developed and supported and motivated through both extrinsic and intrinsic means.

19.0 A focus on changing the way teachers teach will similarly align with a greater emphasis on Inclusive Education. Quality education must be accessible for all UNRWA students and to this effect the importance of an Inclusive Education approach, supported by a Policy, and the development of diagnostic and learning tools to identify, and support children, with Special Education Needs (SEN)—whether they are children who are highly able, or those with learning needs or physical disabilities is key.

20.0 Curriculum support and provision of enrichment materials will complement the teacher development approaches. Curriculum Frameworks will support conceptual sequencing, the instilling of values, ethics and principles of equity and neutrality. Enrichment material will be produced for the UNRWA Human Rights Conflict and Tolerance programme and complemented by targeted teacher training. Ongoing formative student assessment by the teacher will be encouraged to ensure that appropriate and timely intervention and support is given to learners.

21.0 Technical Vocational Education and Training is of increasing importance for UNRWA in a region which is striving to further enhance human development and regional efficiency and productivity, whilst having a high proportion of youth and increasing levels of unemployment. TVET needs to focus on providing relevant technical and professional courses to a growing number of students, particularly those from vulnerable groups. TVET programmes must therefore be market orientated in the immediate, short term and make long term projections, for example with regards to issues such as natural resource management.

22.0 Underpinning all interventions towards effective, quality, relevant and efficient education system is knowledge and understanding of challenges, opportunities and programmatic impact. To this effect the Education Reform places strong emphasis on building the capacity of the UNRWA education cadre to understand the implications of existing research in terms of their work in the education programme. Further to have the ability to identify where UNRWA specific research is required, have the capacity to manage such research, and to be able to reflect the findings in their programmatic planning.

23.0 Each Reform dimension must be aligned with the overall Governance and policy frameworks. The UNRWA Reform will ensure that a clear, coherent Education Governance Framework with corresponding Education Technical Instructions (ETIs) is in place. This Framework will similarly align with Agency—wide Frameworks and Policies.

24.0 The interrelationship of the eight dimensions of the Reform is therefore fundamental to its rationale, design and implementation model. The substantive areas of reform (teacher development, curriculum and student assessment, inclusive education and TVET) are supported by enabling frameworks, evidence based policies, capacity development, governance structures, effective communication and advocacy practices, partnerships and ongoing monitoring and evaluation.

25.0 With regard to overall costs of implementing the Reform, the estimated figure for the five year period is $4 million. Although existing education systems and structures will be harnessed and strengthened there will be strong need for an initial outlay of costs. This will be required for the production of teacher training and TVET materials and implementation models, evidence based policies, frameworks and for monitoring and evaluation. The development of blended learning materials for the training of teachers, Headteachers and education support cadres will consume the largest proportion of the costs.

26.0 Although there will be no additional staff costs in implementing the Reform, as Headquarters and Fields education staff will be actively deployed throughout, however capacities will need to be built. Introducing different ways of managing the education system does have the potential for savings, for example the introduction of new inclusive classroom and school practices will lead to decreased expenditure on `remedial' teaching to students after school hours and in the holidays.

27.0 It is likely that enhanced ICT infrastructure may be required in some Fields to facilitate the Agency wide school based Educational Management Information System (EMIS) and Online Library and Resource Bank. However, the effective delivery of the Education Reform is not dependent upon a sophisticated ICT infrastructure, and the model of implementation of different elements of the Reform can be contextualised to some extent.

28.0 With regard to recurrent costs, one main cost will be the sustained implementation of the Teacher Policy, which will professionalise the teaching and education support at all levels—i.e. through recruitment processes, career progression and ongoing professional development. Its implementation should however allow for more effective deployment of the teaching and educational support staff in the future.

29.0 In summary, the Reform is designed to establish a strong enabling environment, whereby schools and teachers receive appropriate, timely professional and administrative support. Decisions are evidence based are in place and embodied in a comprehensive set of education policies and frameworks. This enabling environment will facilitate educationally, technically and economically meaningful progress towards the achievement of quality education for Palestine refugees. The Reform objectives are in line with the overall UNRWA Sustaining Change agenda, Medium Term Strategy and national, regional and global Education For All aspirations.

30.0 Education reform is an imperative not an option. The current system of education needs to be of higher quality, greater effectiveness, increased efficiency and enhanced equity. It is not serving its ultimate beneficiaries, the Palestine refugees, as it should, by preparing them to develop their full potential to contribute to individual, societal, regional and global development.

Education Programme Reform Log Frame

Intervention Logic	Indicators	Sources of Verification	Assumptions
Reform Goal An UNWRA education programme which develops the full potential of Palestinian refugees **Reform Outcome** To ensure effective, efficient and quality education systems and structures **Reform Outputs**	Pupil survival rates (disaggregated by boys and girls and cycles); Student achievement in MLA (disaggregated by boys and girls and cycles); Percentage of students employed after one year of completing studies (disaggregated by boys and girls and cycles); Students attending remedial programmes (disaggregated by boys and girls and cycles)		
1.1 Professional, qualified and motivated teaching force and empowered schools in place	1.1 All teachers qualified by 2015; All teachers professionally accredited by 2015; Systems of profession development in place by end of 2012	1.1 Human Resources Department (HRM databases, Teacher Policy); EMIS; UNRWA Education Annual Report	
1.2 Equal access for all children to quality education regardless of gender, abilities, disabilities, impairments, health conditions and socio-economic status assured.	1.2 Inclusive systems and structures developed and in place by 2015; inclusive practices adopted in all UNRWA fields of operation by 2015	1.2 Education Department (Annual Report, Inclusive Education Policy); Field Office education programme assessments	Stable political and security environment in host countries

(Contd....)

Intervention Logic	Indicators	Sources of Verification	Assumptions
1.3 Relevant and quality Technical Vocational Education and Training structures/ programmes in place	1.3 Percentage of students employed appropriately; Percentage of students with increased means of livelihood	1.3 EMIS (PCG database); UNRWA Education Annual Report	
1.4 Curricula to support holistic approach to learning and personal development strengthened	1.4 Standards in place for core subject curricula by 2013; Unified tests undertaken biannually (i.e., 2012 and 2015)	1.4 Curriculum Standards Handbook; UNRWA Education Annual Report; EMIS (GEP database)	UNRWA management, staff, host governments and development partners support reform plans
1.5 Evidence based policy making and informed decision-making at all levels in place	1.5 EMIS generated data is used to plan and review Field Implementation Plans (FIPs) and UNRWA Education Annual Report	1.5 EMIS; UNRWA Education Annual Report; Compendium of Educational Research	
1.6 Effective educational governance system at all levels in place	1.6 All Educational Technical Instructions (ETIs) updated by 2015; Degree of compliance with governance systems	1.6 UNRWA Education Annual Report	Adequate funding for implementation of reform
1.7 Education Programme planning management and strengthened	1.7 Common education monitoring frameworks produced to monitor and evaluate education programme implementation	1.7 UNRWA Education Annual Report; Biennium Plan Field Implementation Plans; Handbook of Common Programme Monitoring	
1.8 Partnerships, communication and use of education ICTs strengthened	1.8 % of completed implementation of identified ICT tools by 2015; Partnership and Communication Strategy evaluated by 2015	1.8 UNRWA Education Annual Report; Evaluation of Partnership and Communication Strategy	Capacity and competencies at all levels are sufficient to implement reform programme

For EMIS, GEP refers to the General Education Programme database and PCG refers to the Placement and Career Guidance database

All indicators shall be gender and cycle disaggregated

Baselines and targets to be provided and established, respectively

Chapter 1

Origin and History of Reform Strategy

1.0 In pursuant to the United Nations General Assembly resolution 302 (IV) of 8 December 1949 the United Nations Relief and Works Agency for Palestine Refugees in the Near East (UNRWA) became operational on 1st May 1950. Mandated with responding to the needs of approximately 750,000 Palestine refugees, the Agency's mission is' to help Palestine refugees achieve their full potential in human development under the difficult circumstances in which they live'. The Agency, through its sixty-one years of existence has been fulfilling its humanitarian and human development mandate by providing services to Palestine refugees in the Gaza Strip, the West Bank, Jordan, Lebanon and the Syrian Arab Republic. These services include basic education in all fields (and the additional provision of secondary education in Lebanon), comprehensive primary health care, emergency relief, social interventions, microfinance, and infrastructural support. UNRWA is unique among United Nations agencies, being the longest project in operation and delivering services directly to beneficiaries. With sixty-one years of experience, employing almost 30,000 staff (including 17,246 teachers and 587 vocational training instructors), the majority of whom are Palestine refugees themselves, and catering to 4.82 million Palestine refugees registered with the Agency (June, 2010), it is one of the United Nations largest programmes.

1.1 Since the initial years of conflict sixty years ago, UNRWA has been the main provider of basic education to Palestine refugees. All Palestine refugee children are eligible to avail themselves of the Agency's nine to ten years of free basic education provided in the five Fields of operation and also to secondary schooling in Lebanon. The education programme is the largest of the UNRWA programmes, both in terms of staff engaged and the budgetary allocation. UNRWA education staff comprises more than 70% of the total agency staff and education expenditure accounts for 59 % of the total regular budget. In terms of a single agency managed system, UNRWA operates one of the largest school systems in the Middle East, covering five countries.

1.2 The vision of UNRWA's education programme is to establish:

> *"An UNRWA education system which develops the full potential of Palestine Refugees to enable them to be confident, innovative, questioning, thoughtful, tolerant and open minded, upholding*

human values and religious tolerance, proud of their Palestine identity and contributing positively to the development of their society and the global community".

In achieving its vision, the Agency operates 691 schools across the five Fields of operation providing basic education to around 48% of eligible Palestine refugee children (another 24% attend governmental and private schools). UNRWA also provides limited support to youth, through regular and short term continuing education and skills training programmes offered in its ten Vocational Training Centres (VTCs).

1.3 As the Agency moves forward, there are both external and internal constraints that may impact on the effective implementation of the Reform programme. The external constraints include the political uncertainty in the region, problems of personnel travel and transportation, especially between Gaza and other Fields, and the possible diminishing of donor funding. Internal constraints include limited resources and challenges of developing appropriate structures, and clarifying new roles and relationships in line with the Organisational Development (OD) decentralisation process and the expectations of the Reform process. At Field level the challenges within this context are the planning for the provision of effective services to an increasing client base, yet with limited resources. In this regard, it is key to ensure that the Education Programme is strategically determined and appropriately prioritised, reflecting international standards and good practice. The challenges, however, will also provide opportunities to work together as an Agency in raising the standards of educational delivery and achievement.

1.4 As a prelude to the UNRWA reform initiative, a detailed external review of the education programme was undertaken during 2009. The review highlights that the current system of education needs to be of higher quality, greater effectiveness, increased efficiency and enhanced equity. Its findings aligned with the perceptions of a diverse range of stakeholders whereby UNRWA education is seen as not serving its ultimate beneficiaries, the Palestine refugees, as it should, by preparing them to develop their full potential to contribute to their individual, societal, regional and global development. The reform of the UNRWA Education Programme is thus an imperative not an option.

Chapter 2

The External Environment: Global, Regional & National Analysis & Background of Education

2.1. Palestine refugees in context

2.1.1. UNWRA serves a population of almost 5 million registered refugees across a wide geographical range: Lebanon, Syria, Jordan, West Bank and Gaza. The Agency delivers services in education, health, micro-finance, infrastructure, relief and social services. The design and delivery of these services seek to achieve a balance between overall coherence and strategic frameworks and policies and contextualisation, which reflects political, social and economic contexts that define the refugee situation.

2.1.2. There are common regional trends that inform UNRWA's work. The most significant is a high population growth and a growing youth bulge. Projected demographic changes indicate an increase in demand for education, particularly at the secondary and tertiary level. In Gaza, for example, an additional 120 schools are already needed to cater for the growing school age population, even with 80% of current schools working double shifts to accommodate students (Save the Children 2010d).

2.1.3. Regional political developments also may have considerable, and unfortunately unpredictable, operational consequences for the Agency. Dramatic changes on the political landscape of a number of Arab countries have already begun to have an effect on host countries and will invariably have repercussions for Palestine refugees and UNRWA.

Jordan

2.1.4. Jordan was ranked 96 of 182 the 2009 UNDP Human Development Index (HDI). Through consistent spending on education and development, Jordan has achieved significant poverty reduction, with the incidence of poverty shrinking from 21% in 1997 to 14% in 2003 (World Bank 2010). Alongside this poverty reduction, Jordan has achieved high levels of gender parity in access to basic services (World Bank 2008a), although the inevitable increased strain on such services caused by population growth will need to be addressed in order to maintain these levels in the coming years.

2.1.5. The 1.95 million Palestine refugees in Jordan represent 42% of all registered refugees in the Near East. Most were granted Jordanian nationality in 1954. This entitlement is not extended to 136,000 ex-Gazans, who arrived following the 1967 war and continue to have limited access to higher education, secondary health care, employment and property ownership.

2.1.6. As most Palestine refugees enjoy citizenship, there is no distinction made between refugees and non-refugees in official statistics. An estimated 13% of the population live under the poverty line. Broad government availability of services for Palestine refugees due to their citizenship status is unique to Jordan. For example, 60% of registered refugees attend government schools.

2.1.7. Jordan has experienced strong economic growth in recent years, averaging 7.7% growth per annum between 2004 and 2007, and an estimated rate of 5.5% growth in 2008 (World Bank 2010b). This economic development has been attributed to export-led growth, manufacturing expansion, increased Foreign Direct Investments from oil-rich Gulf States and a construction boom fuelled by increasing real estate prices. Structural reform (namely liberalisation of trade, a privatisation programme, upgrading of regulatory frameworks in key areas such as water and energy) and fiscal consolidation have occurred concurrently (World Bank 2010b, World Bank 2008).

2.1.8. Nonetheless, there have also been economic challenges, particularly the rising oil prices which have put pressure on inflation rates, geographically uneven development, and the impact of the influx of Iraqi refugees. Jordan has a 40% labour market participation rate (one of the lowest in the region), creating a total workforce of 1.4 million (World Bank 2010b). Seventy-five percent of all workers are in the service sector, 22%

in industry and only 3% in agriculture. Government employment accounts for 30% of all jobs, and half of all remaining jobs are accounted for by micro-enterprises (World Bank 2010b), 94% of which employ four workers or fewer (UNRWA 2010c). As a result of the 'youth bulge' described in section 1.2, over 60,000 citizens are entering the labour market each year (World Bank 2010b).

2.1.9. With unemployment levels high (currently at 14%), particularly amongst the young (World Bank 2010b), and costs continuing to rise (UNRWA 2009), catering for these new labour market entrants is one of Jordan's principal economic challenges. Many of the jobs that are created require low-skilled workers, and Jordanians have proved reluctant to take such roles. These jobs often go to migrant workers, who constitute between 20% and 30% of the total work force (World Bank 2008). This, along with the large number of expatriate workers, can create tensions between communities, and it is clear that Jordan needs to create more high productivity jobs, both to cater for its own citizens, and in order to compete in an increasingly knowledge-driven global economy. The impact of the global financial crisis on Jordan has not yet been closely analysed, but the World Bank (2010b) anticipates that it is likely to be negative, with latest estimates for GDP growth in 2009 down to 2.4% (IMF 2010).

Lebanon

2.1.10. Lebanon's HDI score of 83 is the highest in the region, placing it just inside the 'high human development' category. This high score, however, provides a sharp contrast to the marginalized and impoverished existence of the Palestine refugees in the country.

2.1.11. There are approximately 439,000 on UNRWA's official rolls in Lebanon, but a recent American University of Beirut survey puts the number of current residents at 260,000 to 280,000. Palestine refugees in Lebanon are a precarious position as they remain excluded from over 30 professions, may not own or inherit property, and suffer restrictions on their mobility. In 2007, armed conflict led to the destruction of Nahr al-Bared Camp, displacing 26,000, many of whom still live in temporary shelters as UNRWA's reconstruction project continues to suffer severe financial constraints.

2.1.12. Lebanon is the only field in which UNRWA provides secondary education, as it is not available to Palestine refugees otherwise. UNRWA's inability to adequately support the needs of refugees for increasingly expensive tertiary care is the source of considerable hardship to the refugees and ongoing tensions between the Agency and its beneficiaries.

2.1.13. Although Lebanon's parliamentary paralysis has meant that many proposed economic, political and social reforms have been at something of a standstill, the economy has proved fairly robust in the light of the global financial crisis, with GDP growth of between 5% and 7% in 2009 (EC 2010). This is in part attributable to the flexible structure of the economy, which is composed almost entirely of small and medium-sized companies, and the solidity of the banking sector (ETF 2010a). The principal driver of this growth, however, has been increased capital inflow, predominantly due to post-global crisis regional portfolio shifts. Concurrent heightened interest-rate spreads on international markets led to an increase in foreign deposits in Lebanese banks due to its reputation as a relatively safe investment destination (EC 2010). This capital inflow, which may reduce as the world recovers from the financial crisis, has helped to mitigate the serious impact of the dwindling remittances from the financial-crisis affected Lebanese Diaspora, which had accounted for 24% of GDP in 2007 (EC 2010).

2.1.14. Despite this cushioning of the effects of the global financial crisis, Lebanon has still experienced significant increases of up to 17% in the cost of basic services such as education, transport, water and electricity in the last year (EC 2010). The political stalemate and past conflicts have also had a notable negative impact on what had been one of the most promising business sectors in the region (ETF 2010a). Officially, the country has one of the lowest economic activity rates in the Mediterranean region (43% in 2007), although this statistic may in part be a result of the very active informal economy, and an under-declaration of women's participation in the labour force, particularly in rural areas (ETF 2010a). The unemployment rate is between 15% and 20%, and the majority of those affected are first-time job seekers, with 15 - 24 year olds accounting for 45% of the unemployed (ETF 2010a). There is a shortage of job opportunities for people with intermediate qualifications, leading many skilled Lebanese to search for work abroad.

2.1.15. Concurrently, migrant workers often take low skilled jobs, and although a decree for the regulation of employment agencies recruiting migrant workers was passed in January 2009, implementation of measures intended to protect migrant workers from exploitation and abuse remains weak (EC 2010). The service sector contributes 70% of GDP, with the combined industry and manufacturing contributions shrinking to 11.4% in 2006 (ETF 2010a). However, the tourism sector is experiencing something of a revival, and there are several proposals pending that may help to improve the business climate. These include the establishment of one-stop shops in post-offices to help people to set up their own businesses, and making the company register available on-line (EC 2010).

Syria

2.1.16. Syria ranks 107 out of 182 in the HDI, placing it just above the occupied Palestinian territory and in the `medium human development' category (ETF 2010b). Syria hosts between 1 and 1.4 million Iraqi refugees (CIA 2010), alongside nearly 500,000 registered Palestine refugees .

2.1.17. Palestine refugees in Syria do not have citizenship, but do enjoy a broad range of rights, with some restrictions on property ownership. While government services are open to refugees, this access is implicitly qualified by the expectation that the UNRWA maintain universal access to refugees of its services.

2.1.18. Syria has recently improved its economic output performance, with a positive growth of GDP to 7% in 2008. However, economic challenges remain, with inflation rising 15% to 18% in 2008 (ETF 2010b). Services contribute to more than 50% of Syrian GDP, industry to 27% and agriculture to 23%. The public sector is the main employer, accounting for 30% of the employed workforce (compared with 11% globally and 9% in Europe) (ETF 2010b). In contrast, the government views the private sector as the principal vehicle for economic growth and human capital development, implying the need for significant labour market reform. The government's 11th Five-Year Plan, emphasises this, and aims at preparing Syria for a knowledge-based market economy. (ETF 2010b). Although Syria's unemployment rate is slightly lower than Jordan's at 9%, both countries face similar challenges in this area. As in Jordan, youth unemployment is particularly high, and here, the `youth bulge' means that the work force is anticipated to grow by 250,000 to 300,000 people per annum for the next 20 years (ETF 2010b).

2.1.19. To a certain extent, Syria has been somewhat protected from the impact of the global financial crisis due to its limited integration with global financial institutions. However, it will inevitably be affected by falling remittances (Save the Children and CFBT 2010) and high numbers of recently redundant workers returning from affected Gulf States. The European Training Foundation (2010b) estimates that Syria will need to re-integrate around 300,000 returning workers. Syria's foreign aid is also likely to decrease because of the recession, as key donor governments make cuts. Additionally, although new gas reserves have been discovered, the country may exhaust its oil reserves in the near furure, which will further complicate the economic situation (ETF 2010b). As in Jordan, Syria is experiencing continued pressure from the influx of Iraqi refugees who are adding to the substantial and active informal workforce.

Occupied Palestinian Territory (oPt)

2.1.20. The oPt HDI score of 110 is the lowest of UNRWA's fields of operation, and can be attributed to decades of crippling occupation and economic isolation.

2.1.21. Gaza has suffered acute and extensive social and political devastation as a result of occupation and closure. The lack of functioning border crossings has had a significant negative impact on the access for both people and of vital goods, including those necessary for humanitarian operations, with current aid flow into Gaza approximately 25% of the level it was prior to the Israeli blockade imposed in 2007 (Save the Children 2010d).

2.1.22. The prolonged closure of Gaza combined has had an extreme impact on the socioeconomic situation, bringing public services and the private sector close to collapse (UNRWA 2009b). The overall poverty rate in the oPt is 57%, and it is estimated that 80% of people in Gaza live below the poverty line (EC 2010b). The blockade, which has now been imposed for three years, means that an estimated three-quarters of Gaza's population depend on food aid to survive, and an increasing number of Palestinian children are malnourished, anaemic or with vitamin A deficiencies (Save the Children 2010d. After Israel's destructive military operation "Cast Lead" in early 2009, food insecurity rose from 56% to 75% (UNRWA 2009b), and 997,500 Palestinian children are now estimated to be living without adequate food, water or medical attention. Damage to infrastructure means tons of sewage are pumped into the sea each day. Education remains severely disrupted after more than 280 schools were either damaged or completely destroyed by Israeli attacks. (Save the Children 2010d).

2.1.23. Ongoing movement restrictions and the continuing occupation have also had a severely destructive impact on the quality of life in the West Bank (UNRWA 2009c). Lives continue to be disrupted due to house demolitions, forced evictions, land confiscation threats, and loss of livelihoods. (Save the Children 2009). Forty nine percent (49%) of households surveyed in high risk areas of the West Bank said that humanitarian assistance from international organisations was not available, compared to 12% in high risk areas of Gaza (Save the Children 2009

2.1.24. GDP in the oPt remains significantly below levels a decade ago, and the region suffers from widespread acute poverty (EC 2010b).

2.1.25. The economic situation in Gaza has been precarious for years. Hamas' victory in the 2006 parliamentary elections led to further economic decline, as many Western donors suspended direct budgetary support to Gaza. Concurrently, Israel froze Palestinian VAT and customs revenue transfers. The combination of these factors created a fiscal crisis that left the Hamas government with limited ability to pay salaries and provide services (Samhouri 2006).

2.1.26. The recent blockade and conflict with Israel have further worsened the situation. Gaza's industrial and business facilities were severely damaged in the recent war, and sustained private sector activity is yet to be resumed (UNRWA 2009b). Indeed, apart from the impact of diminishing remittances, the oPt as a whole is believed to have been less affected by the global financial crisis than by the Gaza conflict, as a result of which public confidence in the Gazan banking system has been severely undermined. GDP growth rose to 1% in 2009, from -5% in 2008, although population growth means that this still indicates continuing per capita decline (EC 2010b). The progress that has been made is largely due to expansion of the construction, social services and services industries. At the end of 2009, unemployment rates were high, at 39.3% (EC 2010b), and legitimate commercial trade with the outside world remains practically impossible due to the Israeli blockade.

2.1.27. When data becomes available, experts predict that GDP growth in the West Bank will have risen to 7% in 2009 from 5% in 2008. Although not as dramatic as in Gaza, unemployment rates in the West Bank are also high, at 18.1%.

2.1.28. Although a degree of progress was also made related to internal movement of goods within the West Bank, the situation regarding external movement remains unchanged. Significant delays at the commercial crossing points between Israel and the West Bank continue to the detriment of trade due to high costs incurred by traders, particularly around Tarqumiya (EC 2010b).

2.2. Global, regional and host country education policy frameworks

2.2.1. Definitions and understandings about human development have changed considerably over the years since the United Nations (UN) was established. From an initial narrow focus on national economic development and achieved levels of personal income, beliefs about what constitutes worthwhile human development have now broadened to include a much wider range of goals involving the expansion of human freedoms, social choices and opportunities to live a valued, creative and fulfilling life. The UN now describes human development as:

> *"a process of enlarging people's choices. Enlarging people's choices is achieved by expanding human capabilities.... At all levels of development the three essential capabilities for human development are for people to lead long and healthy lives, to be knowledgeable and to have a decent standard of living. If these basic capabilities are not achieved, many choices are simply not available and many opportunities remain inaccessible. But the realm of*

human development goes further: essential areas of choice highly valued by people, range from political economic and social opportunities for being creative and productive to enjoying self respect, empowerment and a sense of belonging to a community" (MTS 2010:15-16).

2.2.2. In this context, eight Millennium Development Goals (MDGs) were agreed at the UN Millennium Summit in 2000. Education is the direct focus of MDGs 2 and 3 and an implicit requirement in achieving the other goals.

- Goal 2: Ensure that, by 2015, children everywhere, boys and girls alike, will be able to complete a full course of primary schooling
- Goal 3: Eliminate gender disparity in primary and secondary education, preferably by 2005, and in all levels of education no later than 2015

2.2.3. The final declaration of the 2000 Summit affirmed these goals, stating that "Education is development. It creates choices and opportunities for people, reduces the twin burdens of poverty and diseases, and gives a stronger voice in society" (UN 2000). The World Education Forum in Dakar, Senegal, in April 2000 saw the adoption of the Dakar Framework for Action, reaffirming the global commitment to achieve Education for All (EFA) by 2015. The task of monitoring and reporting progress on EFA is undertaken by the Education For All Global Monitoring Report team, based within UNESCO. The number of out-of-school children in the world has decreased by more than 40 million since 2000, and there are now 69 million children out of school (GMR 2010b).

2.2.4. However, UNESCO reports that progress is waning, and now projects that by 2015 there will be more children out of school than there are in 2010 (GMR 2010b). One mechanism working to prevent this is the EFA Fast Track Initiative (FTI), formed in 2002 and the first ever global compact on education. The FTI exists as a partnership between donor and developing countries and operates in 42 low income countries, but does not include any of UNRWA's host countries. However, the establishment of the International Network for Education in Emergencies (INEE), and the UN resolution passed on education in emergencies on 9 July 2010 (INEE 2010) have helped to raise the profile of education both in emergencies and conflict-affected fragile states.

2.2.5. The MENA region in general has made significant progress in increasing enrolment levels in recent years. However, this has led to strains within the education sector, due to the subsequent new demands for instruction at post-compulsory levels of education and rising maintenance costs of the established education structures and systems. Education systems across the region are also characterised by ongoing inefficiencies: dropouts, low graduate employment, and globally average learning outcomes. The progress made in increasing access to education has not led to the development outcomes in the region that many had anticipated. The projected figure for out-of-school youth in the MENA region in 2015 is 13 million, many of whom will be from the most vulnerable groups of children—the disabled, the rural, those who speak minority languages, girls, those with health problems and those caught up in violence (World Bank 2008b). This will leave the region far from achieving Education for All by 2015.

2.2.6. Noting the above concerns around achievement of the MDGs by 2015, access-particularly for vulnerable, marginalised groups and for children with special educational needs—does remain a major concern, but the most significant new challenges facing the region centres on quality of educational provision. A key challenge for the MENA region is to create an education system able to compete in the knowledge based economy. The region is increasingly demanding a well-educated, technically skilled workforce producing highvalue-added, knowledge-intensive goods and services (World Bank 2008b). This implies that a growing focus on enquiry-based and proactive learning, group work and creative thinking is needed in the classroom, and MENA countries are also starting to prioritise science and the learning of other languages.

2.2.7. However, despite these aspirations, El-Haichour (2005) found that the main activities in MENA classrooms are copying from the blackboard and listening to teachers, and that even where child-centred teaching methodologies have, supposedly, been introduced, frontal teaching and associated rote-based learning is still dominant. Many MENA countries, including those in which UNRWA operates, are in the initial stages of implementing new and developing existing education policies, and, following a brief overview of key statistics for each country, the key areas of education reform and priority for each country are examined below.

2.3. Host country education analysis

Key education statistics by host country (Source: Global Monitoring Report, GMR 2010)

Jordan

- Compulsory education between ages of 6—16
- Adult literacy rate 92%
- 33% of children enrol in pre-primary (increased from 26% in 1999)
- The Net Enrolment Rate (NER) in primary education is 89% (decreased from 91% in 1999)
- There is an even gender split with regard to NER—with 89% of girls enrolling and 88% of boys and a GPI of 1.02.
- There are 53,000 out of school children in the country
- Of those that enrol, 99% survive in school to the last grade of primary
- In 2002, the pupil to teacher ratio was 20:1
- There is no record of % of trained teachers
- The total public expenditure on education as % of GNP was 5.0% in 1999 (most recent figures

available). This is higher than average for the region but still falls short of the 6% that the OECD recommends for achieving optimal growth.

Syria

- Compulsory education between ages of 6–14
- Adult literacy rate of 84%
- 9% of children enrol in pre-primary (increased from 8% in 1999)
- NER in primary education of was 95% in 2002 (UIS data) (increased from 92% in 1999)
- In 2002, gender parity in primary education NER had not yet been achieved, with 97% of enrolment for boys and 92% for girls and a GPI of 0.95 (UIS data)
- Of those that enrol, 93% survive in school to the last grade of primary (UIS data, 2008)
- Pupil to teacher ratio of 18:1 (decreased from 25:1 in 1999)
- In 2002, 88% of teachers had received the required training
- The total public expenditure on education as % of GNP was 4.9% in 2008. This is higher than average for the region but still falls short of the 6% that the OECD recommends for achieving optimal growth
- No figures for trained teachers were available.

Lebanon

- Compulsory education between ages of 6—15
- Adult literacy rate of 90%
- 74% of children enrol in pre-primary (increased from 58% in 1999)
- NER in primary education is 90% (decreased from 91% in 1999)
- There is an even gender split with regard to NER, with a NER of 89% for girls and 91% for boys and a GPI of 0.98.
- There are 40,000 out of school children in the country
- Of those that enrol, 92% survive in school to the last grade of primary (UIS data, 2008)
- Only 13% of teachers have received the required training
- Pupil to teacher ratio of 14:1
- The total public expenditure on education as % of GNP was 2.2% in 2008 (latest figures available). Although this is an increased from 2% in 1999, it remains a significant under-investment (below OECD 6% guidelines)

oPt

- Compulsory education between ages of 6—15
- Adult literacy rate of 94%

- 26% of children enrol in pre-primary (decreased from 34% in 1999)
- The NER in primary education is 75% (decreased from 97% in 1999)
- The NER is the same for boys and girls (GPI = 1.00)
- There are 110,000 out of school children in the country
- Of those that enrol, 98% survive in school to the last grade of primary (UIS data, 2008)
- There is a pupil to teacher ratio of 29:1 (decreased from 38:1 in 1999)
- 100% of teachers have received the required training
- No figures for total public expenditure on education as % of GNP were available.

Specific policy areas emerging as important in the region

Teacher Education

2.3.1. The development and reform of teacher education is receiving significant attention throughout the region. In Jordan, two major World Bank funded projects (ERfKE I and II—Education Reform for Knowledge Economy) have had large teacher education reform components. The first project ran until January 2009, and alongside delivering intensive teacher training, its outputs included developing new curriculum and teacher guides, learning resource materials and learning assessment tools for all subjects. Key lessons learned, following a review of ERfKE I, included the need for a greater focus on teachers themselves as the key agents of change, rather than on the new materials or methodologies.

2.3.2. The review demonstrated that despite making teachers aware of new methods and approaches, there is still a relatively low level of actual use of these new styles in the classroom. The new learning materials that have been provided are often used within the confines of a conventional teaching approach. So then, it becomes clear that unless the focus is on equipping and empowering the teacher to use the new methodologies on a daily basis, the desired pedagogical shift is unlikely to be obtained. ERfKE II will seek to address these issues.

2.3.3. In addition to these World Bank funded projects, Queen Rania has also established a Teachers' Academy, which has been described as one of the latest pillars of Jordan's educational reform (QRTA 2010). The Academy will train teachers to bring textbooks to life, to facilitate group and enquiry-based learning, and also aims to raise the profile of teachers in Jordanian society. The Government of Jordan has also recently established an independent Higher Education Accreditation Committee, which will lead to better quality teacher training as teacher education institutions are increasingly required to comply with new accreditation standards. At a regional level, a centre supporting academic, pedagogical and ICT training for teachers has been established in each of Jordan's governates, with international university partners to help support each centre's organisational development.

2.3.4. Student-teachers in UNRWA's host countries can now also study online, with distance-learning courses in Elementary Education and the Higher Diploma in Education, offered at a recently established branch of the Arab Open University. In Lebanon, regional teacher-training centres delivering tailor-made programmes have also been established, and many master teachers and trainers have just completed a European Union funded programme covering pedagogical and occupational skills and ICT applications (EC 2010a). A World Bank funded programme has facilitated the establishment of a professional development programme enabling school Principals and Training Centre Directors to improve their leadership, motivational and management skills. To date, 450 Principals have been trained, and the highest achievers are now being supported to train other Principals in turn (World Bank 2010c).

2.3.5. The Palestinian Authority has also been concerned with the standard of teacher education for some years. Approximately 1,800 new teachers are trained each year, chosen from approximately 15,000 applicants. The challenge is therefore not a shortage of teachers, but rather the quality of training that is taking place (Nicolai 2007). Thus, in 2008, the oPt launched a Teacher Education Strategy aiming to develop five progressive values in all teachers by 2014.

It anticipates that the strategy will develop teachers who are committed to their students, who have broad as well as specialised knowledge which they transmit using a variety of active learning approaches, who monitor and guide their students' learning, who have a reflective practice and continue to develop professionally, and who work with their colleagues as members of a community of learners.

2.3.6. This vision is the first amongst UNRWA host countries to articulate qualities that teachers should have. In 2008 the Palestinian National Authority also launched an initiative through its Quality Improvement Fund for partnerships to modernise teacher education programmes, and for the first time in the region, is proposing distinct stages in teacher career development. Currently, the region (and UNRWA) recognises only one type of teacher, and most teachers are at the same grade on the salary scale. These new developments in the oPt mean that teachers are now split into the categories of new teacher (under probation for 1—2 years), teacher, first teacher and expert teacher (Universalia 2010). This differentiation in experience levels will likely facilitate more focused continued professional development, and help with the issues of teacher motivation and retention.

Technical and Vocational Education and Training (TVET)

2.3.7. TVET is an area which has been identified for major reform in several of UNRWA's operating contexts. In Syria, 50% of school students are tracked into vocational education after their final primary school exams, entering an inflexible system with no options for reentering the formal school system (World Bank 2008b) (see Annex 1). TVET is currently managed by a multitude of ministries and additional private bodies. There are over 800 training institutions in the country and the field has neither a clear regulatory framework nor professional standards. Assessment is organised by different centres without national coordination (UNRWA 2010c). Although the government has no overall strategic articulated concept for reform of the TVET system as yet, the broad objectives of expanding TVET in light of demographic pressures, improving quality and relevance to labour market needs, developing human resources, and promoting private sector provision have been established. The European Union funded $10 million programme titled "Upgrading the Vocational Education and Training System and Promoting Continuing Training", was launched with a pilot in 2009, and is expected to begin full implementation in 2011. The principal objectives of the plan are to create a TVET system that better matches the needs of the labour market and to improve the qualitative skills of the labour force. A strategy to this end has been developed and is awaiting government approval, along with a five-year plan that aims precisely to bring the labour market and the education system closer together to reduce the aforementioned mismatch between needs and skills (EFT 2010b). Alongside this there is a plan to establish a National Agency for Vocational Education and Training to facilitate greater coordination and regulation, and to roll out an apprenticeship scheme which has been designed and piloted. EU support for TVET in Syria will continue until 2013, and will prioritise interventions which reach the poorest and most rural areas of the country. However, although these plans hold promise the need for an agenda that is shared by all involved bodies, institutions and partners is yet to be fully met.

2.3.8. In the context of Lebanon's National Education Strategy, TVET reform is a major challenge, and initial steps have been taken to prepare a strategic plan. As in Syria, routes between TVET and mainstream education programmes need to be developed (see Annex 1), and TVET needs to be made more attractive to the general public. Significant challenges that are yet to be addressed include developing the capacity of the Directorate General for Vocational Education and Training, and for the vocational training institutions themselves. Further labour market research needs to be undertaken to ensure that graduates are trained in relevant skills and, to the same end, the role of private and social partners in the steering, management and delivery of the TVET system needs to be enhanced.

2.3.9. When Israel returned the oPt's education system to the Palestinians in 1994, TVET accounted for only 4% of formal secondary education, and was focused on preparing young people for low-skilled jobs in the Israeli labour market (MoEHE 1999). The MoEHE developed a ten year National Strategy for TVET in 1998, designed to offer "clear direction for public policy and investment in TVET...including expansion of the system" (Lempinen and Repo 2002:9

in Nicolai 2007:81). The plan was designed "to create a TVET system that is relevant, flexible, effective, accessible, sustainable, and which fulfils its general obligations towards the Palestinian people" (MoEHE 1999). However, it has been argued that these goals have not been met, due to the overly centralised approach taken by the PA, which has meant that the 926 Palestinian NGOs "don't dare move an inch" to implement programmes without going through several levels of time consuming bureaucracy (Nicolai 2007:50). This means that the TVET programme is limited to being carried out in official government schools and centres, and is planned without participation of local communities (Gladwell 2009a).

2.3.10. As in UNRWA's other fields, the market-relevance of the TVET programme also needs to be addressed, and more time spent on labour market analysis. Flexibility too remains an issue in the oPt (see Annex 1). Although graduates of vocational education courses can now choose to continue their tertiary education at community colleges, those who moved into vocational provision straight after primary school do not have this option. Overall, the TVET system is said to lack unity, be unsystematic, fragmented and outdated, with buildings in increasingly bad condition. A new TVET system, which aspires to be market orientated, flexible, accessible, sustainable and with high quality teaching is now under development (UNRWA 2010c).

2.3.11. Jordan allocates approximately 5% of its public spending on education and training to TVET.

Unlike in other areas of education policy, Jordan still lacks a cohesive strategy for TVET, despite the existence of a TVET Council and a TVET Support Fund. However, the need for a strategy encompassing change in TVET governance has been noted in the National Agenda (UNRWA 2010c), and so progress is potentially close to being made. Jordan has identified four strategic priorities for the reform of TVET; first, as with its neighbours, it intends to improve market linkages to increase relevance; second, it will reform the organisation and management of TVET by developing leadership and creating an increasingly devolved structure; third, it will introduce clear occupational standards; and finally, it will use financial and funding incentives to improve system performance (UNRWA 2010c).

Information Communication Technology (ICT)

2.3.12. ICT endeavours are gaining momentum across the region as UNRWA's host countries recognise the growing need to enable their students to develop their technological capacities. The Near East North Africa (NENA) Information Communication Technology in Education Project, which was established in 2005, has worked in all of UNRWA's operating fields, and also in Egypt. The project focused on capacity building amongst teachers, and developing strategic leadership for improving the use of ICT in schools. The project's training programme has been accredited by the MoE in both Lebanon and Jordan, and training manuals in Arabic and English have been developed in all of the participating countries. A core team of trainers has been built in each country, again with the support of the MoEs, and regional links for knowledge sharing have been established (British Council 2010). In addition to this project, Lebanon has established computer classrooms in the majority of mainstream secondary schools in the country, and in all TVET schools.

2.3.13. Jordan in particular is gaining a reputation for progression and innovation in ICT and education. The Jordan Education Initiative (JEI), which uses ICT to transform the learning environment in schools, recently won the UNESCO prize for ICT use in education (UNESCO 2010). The JEI is a model of public-private partnership between technology firms and the government. The initiative has thus far reached 80,000 students and up-skilled teachers in 102 Jordanian schools (JEI 2010). The MoE is also making it mandatory for students to be computer literate, and able to apply their studies in computers to their regular studies, particularly of science and maths (World Bank 2010b). Outputs of Jordan's Education Reform for the Knowledge Economy I programme, which concluded in 2009, included equipping schools with ICT infrastructure and related e-learning resource materials—ecurricular have been completed in five subjects and Jordan aims to connect every public school to a national broadband network. However, despite these pockets of excellence and the intentions of the Government, the World Bank cited limited use of technology as an area of concern in its Project Appraisal Document for the Education Reform for the Knowledge Economy II programme (World Bank 2010b).

Inclusive Education and Special Educational Needs (SEN)

2.3.14. Although the region in general is yet to establish strong educational programmes that meet the needs of marginalised children and those with special educational needs, there is a growing recognition of the need for change. The West Bank and Gaza provide good examples of what UNRWA host countries are, at a minimum, aspiring to achieve in this area. The Palestinian Child Law of 2005 emphasises the government's commitment to provide education and training in special classes, schools or centres that "are linked to the regular education system; are accessible and in proximity to the child's residence; provide appropriate types and levels of education; and have staff who are educationally qualified to educate children according to their needs" (Universalia for UNRWA 2010 NP). The oPt also has separate, special schools for deaf and blind children, and one for physically handicapped children. However, the Universalia review (2010) found that, in practice, potentially less than 10% of children with SEN are receiving appropriate support.

2.3.15. In Jordan, steps forward are also being taken, both in regard to individual schools and overall approaches to teacher training. At the training level, the University of Jordan now offers both pre-service teacher training and graduate degree programmes in special education. At the school level, the Jordan MoE's Directorate of Special Education has established 400 special education resource rooms in schools across the country. Some 18 specific programmes for students with special needs and 17 centres where cognitive and sensory impairment and learning disabilities can be assessed and diagnosed have also been set up. These centres also enable the identification of gifted and talented students, who are often then moved to a higher grade. In addition to this provision within the mainstream education system, Jordan also has a number of special schools for children with more severe disabilities (UNRWA 2010d).

Early Childhood Development (ECD)

2.3.16. Although not as high-profile as the other policy areas discussed in this report, Jordan has attracted international investment to develop this sector, and as such it is worth briefly detailing. The first stage of the country's aforementioned Education Reform for the Knowledge Economy Project, funded by the World Bank (2010b) and now in its second implementation stage, required the initiation of both quantitative and qualitative development of the ECD sector. The sector is now considered to be one of the more dynamic elements of Jordan's education system, and achievements in the field have included teacher training and professional development, curriculum development, standard setting and increased parental involvement. The private sector is still responsible for 90% of ECD provision, and although this figure is high, it is gradually falling (from 95%in 2003), and the setting of standards, along with stronger regulation, has helped the sector begin to mature (World Bank 2010b).

2.4. Priorities for the international non governmental education development sector

2.4.1. A number of key priorities are emerging across the region for the non-governmental education development sector, ranging from those linked to education in emergencies (relevant to Gaza and the West Bank), to the more widely applicable priorities of skills training and the role of education as related to work, child protection, quality, gender and inclusive education.

2.4.2. The raised profile of education in emergencies noted above has also led to an increased awareness of the important role that education can play in Disaster Risk Reduction (DRR) and emergency preparedness. A number of major International Non Governmental Organisations (INGOs) are calling for more resources to be spent on this in the region, and are encouraging MoEs and partner organisations to integrate emergency preparedness into their curricula. One key example of this is Save the Children's work in the West Bank and Gaza, where they have repeatedly drawn attention to the need for education programmes to include emergency preparedness and DRR components, and are implementing this in their own practice (Save the Children 2009, 2010a, 2010b, 2010c). The International Rescue Committee (IRC) also has a focus on education as part of a humanitarian response, and has significant operations in Jordan and the OPT. However, although host country and Palestine refugee children are not excluded from their work, the clear target beneficiaries are Iraqi refugee children (IRC 2010).

2.4.3. Amongst the somewhat broader concerns, work, and education's role in preparing young people for the labour market, is a recurring focus. World Vision and Christian Aid's work in Lebanon prioritise securing the right to work in all professions for Palestine refugees (Christian Aid 2010, World Vision 2010) and through this promote the value of education. Oxfam provides skills training to vulnerable groups, including women and youth and also works with local partners to link job-seeking students with employers in the private sector who need trained workers (Oxfam 2010a). In Jordan, Questscope also emphasises the importance of training young people in market-relevant technical and vocational skills (Questscope 2010).

2.4.4. Inclusive education and the protection of children in their places of education are also INGO priorities. Save the Children's education work links closely with its protection work, aiming to ensure that all Palestinian children are safe from violence (including corporal punishment) and any kind of abuse in their schools (Save the Children 2010b). Save the Children is also championing inclusive education, arguing that education systems that respond to the needs of the most vulnerable children in their communities have a better chance of enabling all children to access, remain and progress in their education (Save the Children 2010c). Islamic Relief is also prioritising inclusive education in the oPt, running a school for deaf children and providing special provision for those suffering from psycho-social distress (Islamic Relief 2010).

2.4.5. Finally, gender and ensuring access and quality for girls remain significant and ongoing issues.

CARE focuses on women's empowerment in the majority of their programmes, particularly with regard to the labour market (CARE International 2010), and Oxfam's policy priority in its education work is gender equality (Oxfam 2010b). The United Nations report to the Committee on the Elimination of Discrimination Against Women (CEDAW) emphasises the difficulties that girls face in accessing education in the OPT. The difficulties are exacerbated for girls living in rural areas, where traditional attitudes concerning female education are compounded by movement restrictions, and for girls living near Israeli settlements, who have reported harassment on their journey to school (UN 2008).

2.5. Donor trends, priorities and the impact of the global financial crisis on education financing

For key donor information by country, see Annex 2.

2.5.1. As a result of the economic crisis it is estimated that 90 million additional people around the world will be pushed into poverty during 2010 (GMR 2010a). In particular, a major concern is that education progress itself may come under threat because of a reduction in finances from domestic revenues, official development assistance and remittances. The degree to which education in a country is affected by the economic turmoil is defined by multiple factors including: integration into financial markets, employment structures, import and export patterns, and pre-existing poverty. Each of these factors plays an important role in defining who is most affected and for how long. Ultimately it is the most vulnerable in the poorest countries that are least equipped to recover, with the current economic crisis compounding pre-existing vulnerabilities. Those who are already poor in UNRWA's operating fields will be less able to adapt to the new environment. host countries (and indeed UNRWA) must guard against a weakening of enrolments and deterioration in learning which will in turn `weaken [their] ability to be competitive when the global economy recovers' (Barrera et al. 2009:2).

2.5.2. However, the overall impact that the global economic crisis is having on education provision will only be felt gradually over the next few years. Some effects will be direct and others will be indirect knock-on effects such as decreased remittances and widespread unemployment in manufacturing. Securing universal access to good quality education is a top global priority in ensuring that the world is able to emerge from the current recession and build a firm platform for long-term sustainable economic and social development (Davies and McGregor 2009, Global Campaign for Education 2010). The same must be the case for UNRWA's host countries and for UNRWA itself. Having a more literate and educated workforce has an unambiguously positive effect on both the earning potential of an individual and the growth rate of a whole nation (IIASA 2008, GMR 2009, OECD 2006, Harmon et al. 2003, Hanushek et al. 2008), and, more than ever, it is of vital importance that UNRWA harnesses this potential for the benefit of the Palestine refugee children in their care.

2.6. UNRWA organisational structures

2.6.1. The Education Reform Strategy (ERS) is developed within the existing UNRWA frameworks which, over the term of the Reform, are outlined as follows:

2.6.2. The MTS provides strategic direction of the programme activities in the Agency over the 2010 - 2015 term. It articulates a set of fifteen Strategic Objectives, in line with the four Human Development Goals which are cascaded across the Agency;

2.6.3. There are three biennia in the six-year period which are operationalised into Field Implementation Plans (FIP) and Headquarter Implementation Plans (HIP). The FIP and HIP documents outline intended outcomes and outputs, each with indicators containing target and baseline values, consistent with the direction set out in the MTS. The documents are integrated with financial resource allocations, budgeted in accordance with Agency guidance notes, and published by the Finance Department and the Programme Coordination & Support Unit (PCSU).

2.6.4. An Agency-wide Organisational Development (OD) project was initiated from 2006 to 2009, introducing the concept of Strategies, Policies, Accountability, Resources and Envelopes (SPARE) and operational decentralization and focusing primarily on the support service structures within the Agency. The project has provided an increased role and greater responsibilities for Field Offices in the implementation of programme activities, with Headquarters leading on strategic direction, policies, frameworks and tools.

2.6.5. Cross-cutting areas were identified, namely gender, disability, youth, environment and protection. These are of great pertinence to the Education programme and as such education issues are addressed in the frameworks and strategies developed in this regard. For example, the Protection Standards adopted by UNRWA which specifically address education. It will be important that work carried out on the cross-cutting themes and the work on the education reform feed into each other.

2.6.6. The UNRWA Sustaining Change project, from 2010, seeks to maintain the changes and improvements realised during the OD process and to focus on the effectiveness and efficiency of programme service delivery. It also seeks to introduce a strategic and purposeful approach to fundraising and forge new and productive partnerships, whilst maximising impact from existing relationships.

Chapter 3

Education in UNRWA

3.1. Overview

3.1.1. This chapter provides a status of educational provision and achievement across UNRWA. The number of refugees served by UNRWA has been growing at about 3% per annum but is now believed to be slowing down. Currently 485,374 (2010/2011) children are attending UNWRA schools, with a further 238,607 (2006/2007) being accommodated in either host government (Jordan, Syria and Lebanon) schools, in the occupied Palestinian territories (oPt) schools in the West Bank and Gaza, or through private sector provision or other private means.

3.2. Elementary, preparatory and secondary education

3.2.1. One of the principal aims of UNRWA'S Education Programme is to provide Palestine refugee children with appropriate knowledge and skills, in line with the Agency's commitment to the Millennium Development Goals (MDGs) and the EFA initiative. The UNRWA school system functioned through dedicated functionaries in each of the fields and with strategic support from the School Development Division (SDD) and the Institute of Education at Headquarters, Amman. The Field and Headquarters structures and systems compliment each other in terms of providing support to the schools and teachers who deal directly with the community and children.

3.2.2. Elementary education provision at UNRWA comprises of six (6) years of schooling for all eligible[1] Palestine refugee children who reach the age of 5 years and 8 months at the beginning of the school year in Jordan and Lebanon, and 5 years and 7 months in West Bank, Gaza and the Syrian Arab Republic.

3.2.3. UNRWA considers preparatory education an integral part of the basic education cycle and it is thus compulsory and free of charge for girls and boys. On successful completion of the elementary cycle, UNRWA students are promoted to the preparatory cycle, which consists of three years in the West Bank, Gaza, the Syrian Arab Republic and Lebanon and four years in Jordan. The Palestinian Authority (PA) has repeatedly requested the introduction of a fourth preparatory year to schools in the West Bank and Gaza, but as yet financial constraints have prevented this from being implemented.

[1] Children of Registered Palestine Refugees / Children of Palestine Refugee married to a non refugee / Children of non Registered Palestine Refugees

3.2.4. Secondary education is offered only in one field, Lebanon. This unique provision was made to address the problem of restricted access for Palestine refugees to government schools in Lebanon, and the prohibitively high cost of private schools. In view of these special circumstances, UNRWA operates eight secondary schools in Lebanon, catering for 3,411 students and employing 233 teachers in 2009/2010.

3.2.5. Post-secondary level education is offered through UNRWA's TVET courses, and in Jordan and West Bank, university level education for teacher training is available through Education Science Faculties. However, in order to facilitate the creation of academic and intellectual leadership in the refugee community, UNRWA provides some project funded scholarships for education which are supported by donors. Scholarships are awarded according to academic merit and are renewed annually for those who demonstrate academic success in their studies. Support to the scholarship programme, through the UNRWA General Fund, was discontinued, creating increased donor dependency, thereby reducing the numbers of scholarships available to be awarded and also, increasing pressure on UNRWA's TVET services.

3.3. Enrolment, premises and double shifts

3.3.1. Over the past decade there has been a considerable increase in the number of schools and the children enrolled in the UNRWA schools.

Table 1 Number of UNRWA schools

Number of UNRWA Schools—by Field (2000—2010)

	Gaza	Lebanon	Syria	Jordan	West Bank	Total
2000/2001	168	76	110	190	95	639
2001/2002	169	79	111	190	95	644
2002/2003	174	84	113	190	95	656
2003/2004	177	86	115	190	95	663
2004/2005	180	87	115	177	93	652
2005/2006	187	87	118	177	94	663
2006/2007	193	86	118	177	92	666
2007/2008	214	83	119	176	94	686
2008/2009	221	81	119	174	94	689
2009/2010	228	75	118	173	97	691

3.3.2. Some 13% of UNRWA's administrative elementary schools and 18.28% of preparatory schools operate from rented premises. These premises are predominantly exresidential units, rather than purpose built schools and as such lack the physical spaces, lighting and ventilation necessary to create an environment conducive to learning. Facilities that enable quality teaching and learning such as libraries, laboratories and playgrounds also tend to be absent. The small classrooms lead simultaneously to overcrowding and increased teacher recruitment, putting pressure on rapidly diminishing resources. These factors, combined with poor infrastructure and an absence of co-curricular and extra-curricular activities, also impact negatively upon both the quality of education provided and the overall development of the children concerned.

Table 2: Number of schools

2009/2010	Number of Administrative Schools	No. of 2009/2010 Number of School Buildings		Total No. of School Buildings
		UNRWA Built Schools	Rented	
Gaza	228	129	-	129
Lebanon	75	39	27	66
SAR	118	55	07	62
Jordan	173	70	25	95
WB	97	82	15	97
Total	**691**	**375**	**74**	**449**

3.3.3. Around 80.4% of elementary schools and 65.3% of preparatory schools continued their operations on a double shift basis (housing two separate administrative schools in one building, working in morning and afternoon shifts), an arrangement required to overcome resource constraints and ensure universal access to basic education for all refugee children.

Table 3: Administrative schools: field, cycle and shift

	Elementary			Preparatory			Secondary*		Grand Total
	Single	Double	Total	Single	Double	Total	Single	Total	
Gaza	11	122	133	17	78	95	-	-	228
Lebanon	17	06	23	32	12	44	08	08	75
SAR	-	64	64	04	50	54	-	-	118
Jordan	03	37	40	14	119	133	-	-	173
WB	25	-	25	71	01	72	-	-	97
Total	**56**	**229**	**285**	**138**	**260**	**398**	**08**	**08**	**691**

* *All the secondary schools in Lebanon are operated on a single shift basis.*

3.3.4. The average classroom occupancy rate in the elementary cycle is currently 36.90 pupils per class. Syria has the highest average classroom occupancy rate with 38.21 pupils per class, and Lebanon the lowest with 30.54 pupils per class. The average classroom occupancy rate in the preparatory cycle is 36.21 pupils per class. Jordan has the highest number of pupils per class (38.90) and Lebanon the lowest (29.89). This corresponds to a decrease by 5.5% at elementary level and 11.00% at preparatory level in the occupancy rate since 2005-2006, but overcrowding remains an issue. Financial constraints have meant that the Agency has had limited ability to employ additional teachers, or to construct new schools and classrooms in order to achieve ideal teacher student ratios.

Table 4: Number of teaching staff employed by UNRWA (2002/03 - 2009/10)*

	Gaza	Lebanon	Syria	Jordan	WB	Total
2002/2003	5444	1542	1818	4382	1975	15161
2003/2004	5786	1589	1974	4407	2058	15814
2004/2005	6015	1609	1996	4375	2128	16123
2005/2006	6330	1722	2193	4790	2249	17284
2006/2007	6397	1725	2219	4623	2238	17202
2007/2008	6604	1705	2283	4794	2291	17677
2008/2009	7493	1633	2302	4799	2238	18465
2009/2010	7661	1745	2299	4811	2456	18972

**Including Headteachers and Assistant Headteachers*

3.3.5. UNRWA's average pupil teacher ratio (PTR) is 31.14d:1 at elementary level, 23.7:1 at preparatory level and 14.64:1 at secondary level. While the average

Agency PTR is comparatively acceptable, there is significant variation between the fields and within the fields between different schools. Drop-out rate in the elementary cycle was relatively stable at around 1.5%, increasing to around 2.9% for boys and 2.31% for girls at the preparatory level.

Host government policies on detentions has led UNRWA to adopt a promotion policy in order to reduce the number of repeaters. This policy has been effective in motivating pupils to remain in school.

3.3.6. With the exception of the Syria and Lebanon Fields, where end-of-cycle state examinations are sat; UNRWA schools conduct their own examinations in the preparatory cycle. Overall, the performance of children in these examinations has been good with the pass rate ranging from 85-95%. At secondary level in 2009/10, the student pass rate in the general secondary examination was high, at 91.89%. This represents a marginal decrease in overall results when compared to the previous year's 93.76% pass rate, attributable predominantly to lower results in Life Sciences.

3.4. Teacher training and development

3.4.1. UNRWA's teacher education programme aims to maintain and improve the quality of education provided to Palestine refugee children in the Agency's schools. To this end, the Agency works to upgrade the professional qualifications of its teaching staff, enabling them to adapt to curriculum changes, improve their teaching methods, and develop their supervisory skills. This has traditionally been achieved through regular in-service training programmes organised by the Institute of Education (IE), UNRWA Headquarters, Amman and implemented by the Education Development Centres in the fields. Since its establishment in 1964 as a joint UNRWA/UNESCO project, the IE has played a pioneering role in training and developing capacities of thousands of teachers, head teachers and supervisors in the Agency's areas of operation. Annually, an average of 800-900 staff receive in-service training covering diverse content and skill areas.

3.4.2. Teacher training at the pre-service level also seeks to ensure that sufficient qualified teachers are available to staff the UNRWA school system and other school systems in the region. The two-year pre-service teacher education programme, which has been offered in Jordan and the West Bank for the past four decades, was upgraded in 1993 to a four-year university level teacher education programme leading to a first university degree. Since then, the programme has been offered at the three UNRWA Faculties of Educational Sciences and Arts (FESA) in Amman (Jordan) and the two Educational Science Faculties (ESFs) in Ramallah (West Bank). In addition, the FESA in Jordan also offered an in-service three-year teacher education programme to help teaching staff upgrade their qualifications from a twoyear diploma to a first university degree in order to meet new standards set by the Government of Jordan and the Palestinian Authority. The three FESA/ESFs accommodate 1,630 students and teachers every year. In response to difficulties faced by the Lebanon Field in recruiting qualified teachers, a two-year pre-service teacher-training diploma, focusing on the first three grades of the elementary cycle was introduced in September 1997 with an intake of 50. In September 1998 the programme was further expanded, doubling the intake to 100 students.

3.4.3. Overall the IE has managed to respond effectively to growing demands and changing needs, not only by adapting contents to needs, but also by following a well developed methodology of training that responds effectively to diversified requirements.

3.5. Technical and Vocational Education and Training (TVET)

3.5.1. In addition to mainstream school education, UNRWA provides alternative educational opportunities through Technical and Vocational Education and Training (TVET). In 1953, the Agency began providing TVET to Palestine refugees by establishing its first Vocational Training Centre (VTC) in Kalandia Camp near Jerusalem.

3.5.2. The TVET sub-programmes offer vocational training to Palestine refugee youths and equip them with skills and technical expertise relevant to host country job markets. The Agency offers TVET courses in both traditional and modern trades (vocational) and professional through its ten VTCs and accommodates approximately 6,650 trainees annually. The two main types of courses offered are:

1. Trade (vocational) courses of one-year duration (Skilled Labourer level) and two year duration (Craftsman level) are offered at post-preparatory school level for those who have successfully

completed nine or ten years of schooling (depending on the system of the host countries)

2. Semi-professional courses of two year duration are offered at the post-secondary school level for those who have successfully completed 12 years of schooling (successful completion of the state examination).

3.5.3. In addition to these regular programmes, TVET centres also offer short-term needsbased training courses in collaboration with NGOs. These courses focus largely on providing employable skills and knowledge at basic and advanced levels.

Table 5: TVET fact sheet—courses offered, training places, training centers (2010)

Training places (2009/2010)	Gaza	Lebanon	Syrian Arab Republic	Jorban	West Bank	Total
Vocational (Craftsman Level) Courses	700	580	300	596	601	2777
Trade Programme (Skilled Labourer Level) Courses	-	28	242	-	-	270
Technical (Semi-Professional) Courses	764	663	650	790	736	3603
Total VTCs Training Places	1464	1271	1192	1386	1337	6650
Instructors of VTCs	146	89	92	169	150	646
Number of training centres	2	2	1	2	3	10

3.5.4. The West Bank field launched its Tertiary Education Reform: Towards a Confident and Self-

Reliant Youth in October 2009 in order to enhance the sustainability of its three VTCs and promote youth development and poverty alleviation. The reform has also resulted in increased partnerships and exchanges of expertise with the private sector, universities, donors and other national and international TVET actors, leading to improved access to job opportunities and internships for graduates.

3.5.5. In the school year 2008/2009 UNRWA's Damascus Training Centre ran a recent pilot project—in the academic year 2008/9—offering one-year training programmes in seven areas of high demand in local job markets using the Competency-Based Training (CBT) approach. The pilot has been well appreciated and the TVET Unit at HQ Amman has begun to replicate the model at other training centres, namely at Gaza, Siblin, North Lebanon and Wadi Seer Training Centres.

3.5.6. UNRWA also provides professional and career guidance for students, and placement services for its graduates. Surveys of UNRWA graduate trainees routinely show high success rates in finding jobs within one year of graduation. Graduates of UNRWA training institutions also tend to achieve very high pass rates in state certifying examinations.

3.6. Gender equity

3.6.1. UNRWA's school system was the first in the Middle East to achieve gender equity in enrolment rates. In 2010, 49.7% of enrolment at elementary cycle comprised of female pupils. The number of female pupils in the preparatory cycle was marginally higher at 50.40% of total enrolment. In 1962, the Agency opened the first women's VTC in the Arab world and today female enrolment in TVET programmes accounts for 36% of total enrolment. This impressive record notwithstanding, gender equality has not yet been achieved in two important areas: the special needs of boys are not being adequately served, and progress in implementing the gender mainstreaming framework has been slow (*finding 12, Quality Education, Universalia*).

Table 6: Student enrolment in UNRWA schools (elementary cycle) disaggregated by gender

		2008/2009	2009/2010	Change	
				Number	%
Gaza	Boys	71811	75941	4130	5.75%
	Girls	64558	67264	2706	4.19%
	Total	**136369**	**143205**	**6836**	**5.01%**
Jordan	Boys	36551	36033	-518	-1.42%
	Girls	36815	36137	-678	-1.84%
	Total	**73366**	**72170**	**-1196**	**-1.63%**
Lebanon	Boys	10369	9905	-464	-4.47%
	Girls	10469	10191	-278	-2.66%
	Total	**20838**	**20096**	**-742**	**-3.56%**
Syria	Boys	23237	23383	146	0.63%
	Girls	21717	22015	298	1.37%
	Total	**44954**	**45398**	**444**	**0.99%**
West Bank	Boys	15773	15561	-212	-1.34%
	Girls	21146	21024	-122	-0.58%
	Total	**36919**	**36585**	**-334**	**-0.90%**

Total	Boys	157741	160923	3182	2.02%
	Girls	154705	156631	1926	1.24%
	Total	**312446**	**317554**	**5108**	**1.63%**

3.6.2. Conversely, in the preparatory cycle, there has been a decrease in the boys' enrolment in almost all fields except Gaza. Although Syria had an overall increase in enrolment of both girls and boys, the percentage of girls enrolled was higher (4.23%) than boys (2.92%). There was an 8.80% decrease in boys' enrolment in Lebanon, a 2.69% decrease in Gaza and a 0.30% decrease in Jordan. Overall, girls' enrolment improved by 0.74% and boys' enrolment decreased by 1.30%.

Table 7: *Student enrolment in UNRWA schools (preparatory cycle) disaggregated by gender*

		2008/2009	2009/2010	Change	
				Number	%
Gaza	Boys	31577	31383	-194	-0.61%
	Girls	30914	31526	612	1.98%
	Total	**62491**	**62909**	**418**	**0.67%**
Jordan	Boys	26323	26109	-214	-0.81%
	Girls	24228	23942	-286	-1.18%
	Total	**50551**	**50051**	**-500**	**-0.99%**
Lebanon	Boys	4390	4283	-107	-2.44%
	Girls	5253	5102	-151	-2.87%
	Total	**9643**	**9385**	**-258**	**-2.68%**
Syrian Arab Republic	Boys	10250	10374	124	1.21%
	Girls	10275	10242	-33	-0.32%
	Total	**20525**	**20616**	**91**	**0.44%**

West Bank	Boys	8293	8109	-184	-2.22%
	Girls	11172	10985	-187	-1.67%
	Total	**19465**	**19094**	**-371**	**-1.91%**
Total	Boys	80883	80258	-625	-0.77%
	Girls	81842	81797	-45	-0.05%
	Total	**162725**	**162055**	**-670**	**-0.41%**

3.6.3. Some 58.43 % of teachers employed in UNRWA schools are female. Gender sensitive issues around appointing female teachers to boys' schools exist, particularly in Jordan, yet with increasingly few men opting to pursue teaching careers, the issue is unlikely to be quickly resolved.

Table 8: Teaching staff by gender (2010)

Field	Male	Female	Total
Gaza	2824	4208	7032
Lebanon	581	771	1352
Syria	859	1385	2244
Jordan	2118	2372	4490
West Bank	839	1412	2251
Total	**7221**	**10148**	**17369**

3.6.4. UNRWA Education Gender Mainstreaming Strategy identified six outputs to achieve in order to reduce the gender gaps and improve the quality of its services:

1. A better balanced workforce achieved;
2. Parity in enrolment maintained and gendered drop-out reasons identified;
3. TVET enrolment and targeting of girls improved;

4. Measures to address gender stereotypes in the curricular implemented;
5. Confidence levels and participation of girls and boys increased;
6. Gender inequality addressed through special projects and curriculum enhancement.

For the next biennium UNRWA education programme prioritised addressing gender stereotypes and the drop out rate.

3.7. Education financing

3.7.1. UNRWA depends predominantly on donor contributions either from the General Fund or for special projects and initiatives. Overall, taking into account refugee numbers, and inflation, there has been a budgetary decline in recent years. Consequently, various austerity measures have been implemented, which have inevitably had a negative impact on quality and service provision. These measures have included reducing overall running costs and lowering increases in teacher pay. The conflict in Gaza and the West Bank and restrictions in Gaza on the importation of teaching, learning and construction materials have further impacted on the system.

Table 9: *Education programme budget allocations (2007-2010)*

Location	2007*	2008**	2009**	2010
HQ (A)	2,873,000	2,145,245	2,199,290	2,346,701
Gaza	95,928,000	91,505,729	92,571,754	132,627,865
Lebanon	39,268,000	33,678,017	34,445,080	37,206,206
SAR	17,675,000	19,046,854	19,172,305	27,174,171
Jordan	72,704,000	64,976,254	66,173,703	74,053,009
WB	48,765,000	39,736,799	40,333,479	48,303,470
Total	**277,213,000**	**251,088,898**	**254,895,611**	**321,711,422**
Budget-Agency Wide	505,673,000	544,649,000	548,603,000	601,916,000
Education %	54.82%	46.10%	46.46%	53.45%

Source: Programme Budget 2006/2007, **Finance Management System

3.7.2. Catering to the education needs of half-a-million children, education is UNRWA's largest programme, both in terms of staff and financial resources. In 2009 some 70% of total Agency staff were educational staff, and educational expenditure accounted for 53% of the Agency's budget. Managing the increasing staff costs and the overall costs per pupil has been a challenge to administrators struggling with deficit budgets. The current Education reform process aims to optimise resources by unifying processes and scaling up initiatives, assisting the fields through the provision of centralised policies, strategies and some training and materials development, and improving communication strategies for better dissemination of good practices.

Table 10: *Education programme budget in US$*

Cost per Pupil - Elementary and Preparatory Cycle (US$)

	Jordan		Lebanon		Syria		West Bank		Gaza	
	Cost Elem	Cost Prep	Cost Elem	Cost Prep	Cost Elem	Cost Prep	Cost Elem	Cost Prep	Cost Elem	Cost Prep
Dec-97	318.0	373.0	447.0	581.0	147.0	205.0	391.0	560.0	270.0	498.0
Dec-98	312.1	363.9	439.4	577.8	134.1	187.4	367.9	506.2	252.9	458.4
Dec-99	315.3	384.8	460.7	572.5	134.5	201.3	332.6	487.0	234.0	425.2
Dec-00	336.2	392.4	460.0	780.2	147.8	207.2	361.7	474.0	253.6	432.2
Dec-01	339.0	384.5	460.6	745.8	143.6	205.4	368.8	475.0	251.1	425.5
Dec-02	335.1	378.2	466.7	724.0	158.2	240.0	401.0	417.7	303.1	582.8
Dec-03	336.2	379.7	463.5	719.4	156.8	237.9	398.6	415.2	304.1	584.7
Dec-04	295.7	414.4	513.0	765.6	207.1	311.4	468.9	507.8	327.0	495.0
Dec-05	-	-	-	-	-	-	-	-	-	-
Dec-06	430.1	452.8	565.5	803.0	209.0	296.9	507.9	615.0	371.8	504.0
Dec-07	407.6	433.6	626.5	965.2	243.5	319.5	582.6	689.1	480.7	635.1
Dec-08	571.2	813.9	757.1	1169.1	306.2	395.5	545.0	534.7	751.5	852.5
Dec-09	572.9	556.2	1035.9	1500.3	372.8	523.8	711.3	853.9	675.0	936.0

* Dec 2005 figures were deleted due to inaccuracies

3.8. Development Partner support

3.8.1. UNRWA and the United Nations Educational, Scientific and Cultural Organisation (UNESCO) have had a unique partnership relationship since 1951, when an agreement was signed committing UNESCO to providing UNRWA with technical education support. This technical assistance continues today, with UNESCO seconding technical and managerial staff to the Agency on a non-reimbursable loan basis.

3.8.2. Alongside the agreement with UNESCO, UNRWA also collaborates with various host governments and donor agencies to enhance the quality of its Education Programme. The TVET programmes in particular have benefited from partnering with a variety of external organisations and institutions, which have provided expertise in capacity building, accreditation, monitoring and evaluation and in-work training for VTC students. It has also been vital for UNRWA to liaise with external agencies in order to ensure the free horizontal and vertical movement of UNRWA students to other education systems. To this end, UNRWA, UNESCO and representatives of the host countries agreed that UNRWA will follow the curriculum and education structure of its host countries.

3.9. Educational challenges

3.9.1. Half of the refugee population is aged under 20, placing huge pressure on UNRWA's schools and VTCs. Despite ongoing efforts to upgrade and expand infrastructure, through the generous donations of various donors, the majority of schools continue, as noted above, to operate in double shifts and in rented premises, many of which urgently need upgrading or replacing. The issue of infrastructure upgrading and expansion is further complicated by both political sensitivities and the temporary status of the Agency, whereby, a number of regulatory constraints are imposed, such as, no authority to purchase land for schools or other purposes. This leaves the Agency overly dependent on its donors in its attempts to provide quality education for all Palestine refugee children.

3.9.2. Providing schooling in conflict and difficult locations is a particular challenge. Ongoing conflict in Gaza has caused damage to school property and interrupted schooling, with students losing school days due to the conflict, and with many also suffering from posttraumatic stress. The blockade has also led to a huge shortage of uniforms, school bags, school supplies and learning materials. Even the provision of basic supplies, such as paper for textbooks, notebooks and chalk was delayed for months. The blockade has also left many parents of UNRWA school children unemployed, leading to extreme poverty and severe food insecurity. In West Bank checkpoints and movement restrictions continue to hinder access to education and the supply of materials, negatively impacting on the quality of schooling provided.

3.9.3. The Agency responded to this situation by prolonging the school year, when allowed to do so by the authorities, and by providing extra classes to compensate for lost instruction time. Hundreds of hours of additional instructional time and remedial classes in each school have, to some extent, begun to compensate for the time lost. Teams of trauma counsellors have also been employed to work with those children who have been emotionally scarred by their experiences. However, despite these significant efforts, it has not been possible to entirely mitigate the negative effects of such lengthy disruptions to children's education.

3.9.4. In Lebanon the poor socio-economic situation and extremely limited access to employment and other facilities, has been affecting the refugee population Despite UNRWA's efforts to provide refugee children with secondary provision, enrolments have been decreasing and the performance of students has been below the National average in preparatory education. While achievement in UNRWA schools is higher than in government schools at the secondary level, this can be related to lower transition rates from preparatory to secondary education in UNRWA schools than in national schools.

3.9.5. These over arching challenges lead to a number of specific educational challenges. Through the Reform, UNRWA seeks to address the various issues and challenges in a collaborative and strategic manner. UNRWA reaffirms its continued commitment to quality education for Palestine refugees, as it designs and develops strategic education innovations to improve its education programmes, and responds to those introduced by the host authorities.

Chapter 4

Overview of the Education Review by Universalia

4.1. Overview

4.1.1. In 2009, UNRWA conducted an organisational assessment of the Education Programme. The assessment took place within the context of the Organizational Development Plan, and was to serve as a basis to inform the next phase of development in UNRWA's education sector, which sought to develop and implement UNRWA-wide reforms. With the assistance of CIDA, a scoping mission was undertaken to define the parameters of a full organizational assessment. The Review was captured in six technical studies:

1. Moving forward after 60 Years: Synthesis of the Assessment of UNRWA's Education Programme;
2. The Quality of UNRWA Education;

3. The Organization and Management of UNRWA Education;
4. The Evolving Nature of UNRWA's Schools (with an Annex on Observations on Human Rights Education Programming);
5. Review and Forward-Looking Assessment of UNRWA Teacher Education;
6. Special Education Programming in UNRWA

4.1.2. This chapter seeks to provide highlights of the recommendations and findings of the Universalia Report. The direct reference in this chapter to the Review is acknowledged from the onset and appreciation of the high quality work of the Review team is evidenced by the, sometimes verbatim, drawing on the Reports. The purpose of the Review was to give UNRWA's Education Programme a clear steer towards Reform and therefore we hope that the direct utilisation of their text highlights the extent to which it has achieved this.

4.1.3. Overall, the Review concluded that UNRWA has a major challenge in providing quality education outcomes for large numbers of Palestine refugees in its five Fields. However, it highlighted that despite a positive reputation historically, stakeholders perceive that quality has declined in all Fields. Academic achievement is comparable to host country levels in Jordan and Syria, but is below host government norms in the other fields. Throughout the system, relatively large numbers of children are not remaining in school for the nine years of basic education that UNRWA attempts to provide, so the observed achievement test results exclude some students. Furthermore, UNRWA is only beginning to provide education services for children with special learning needs. The challenge is to serve a greater proportion of eligible refugees and to ensure that all students have quality education.

4.2. Quality of UNRWA Education

4.2.1. The Review team expressed their awareness of the dedication of Palestinian parents and teachers to the education of their children and students. It states how it is their concerns about the quality of education being provided to Palestine refugee children that have driven the Review. The Review was thus based around key factors identified by parents and teachers as affecting the quality of teaching and learning in UNRWA schools, and therefore impacting on the lives of students, teachers and families.

4.2.2. The Review describes one of the main challenges the programme is facing: the maintenance of quality. A growing refugee population and the consequent increase in enrolments, has led to overcrowded classrooms, higher pupil to teacher ratios than those of host countries, and 77% of schools running on a double shift system. It points out that this is happening at a time when UNRWA's financial resources are diminishing, making it difficult for UNRWA to keep pace with the educational reforms occurring, (as discussed in Chapter 2), in some host countries. Similarly, the Review notes a deterioration in school infrastructure and an increase in the number of schools operating in rented facilities, which means that classrooms are often too small, poorly lit or overly hot or cold. Further, the Review makes reference to the lack of teaching and learning materials, describing much of the furniture and equipment as outdated and in need of repair. It goes on to talk of the reportedly low morale of teaching staff and the needs of children for supportive education and psychosocial support, due to the conditions of poverty and conflict in which many live. One indicator of quality provision is examination results and the Review suggests that recent exams *`have shown shockingly high failure rates'*.

4.2.3. The issue of defining and providing quality education is discussed as is the unusual nature of UNRWA, as both an organization providing direct services in response to emergency and development contexts, and a UN agency, working to build sustainable education capacities in Palestine refugee communities. As a service provider, UNRWA operates within the MENA region, following the host country curriculum and, sometimes, the examination system. Perhaps more importantly however, is the broader social, economic, cultural and economic context of the host countries that any education system is likely to reflect. In the Review this issue is discussed through reference to the Arab Knowledge Report of 2009 which states that although;

> *`Most Arab societies have recorded a number of tangible achievements on the quantitative level in terms of educational opportunities for children and of gender parity, but the qualitative performance of the children of the Arab states as a whole is rarely*

comparable to that of their peers in the rest of the world'. (Arab Knowledge Report, 2009)

4.2.4. The Review highlights some of the limitations of alignment with host country standards and makes reference to other frameworks such as the Inter-Agency Network for Education in Emergencies (INEE) which provides minimum basic standards for emergency contexts, and which the Review describes as emphasizing themes and underpinning principles that are highly applicable to UNRWA. It discusses how the development and application of UNRWA wide standards can help frame policies on quality education whilst allowing for contextualisation.

4.2.5. Two approaches to improving quality are outlined by the Review as follows; (i) to do more of what is already being done with more resources; or (ii) to do more with the resources at hand. Referring to the former, apart from resource constraints, the Review suggests that the system has not sufficiently evolved to current education best practices. Regarding the latter, the need to consider all the possibilities of change is raised, as is the need to focus not only on the outcomes of quality education, but also on how to achieve those outcomes.

4.2.6. With reference to doing more of what is already being done with more resources (high or medium costs but essential), the Review highlights the need to look at:

1. School infrastructure (safety, health, configurations to support modern pedagogy)

2. Specialised services like SEN
3. Qualified and professional teachers as it relates to ESFs
4. School leadership and culture and ethos
5. Student centred model of teaching

It looks then at quality improvements, that is to do more with the resources at hand (low cost), namely to:

1. Generate transparent data on expenditure per pupil
2. Reach international standards on instruction time
3. Improve pupil attendance and timeliness
4. Increase access to current resources
5. Facilitate continuous school improvement (School Quality Review - SQR)
6. Increase monitoring data in key areas like parent surveys, survival rates, unified tests, host government exams and the Trends in International Mathematics and Science Study (TIMMS) raw data
7. Carry out cohesive evaluation and analysis of student learning and programmes, pilots and solution dissemination
8. Reduce heavy course content which requires dialogue with host countries

4.2.7. In the overall pursuit of quality education, the Review discusses the need to focus on basic values related to access, inclusion and equity and suggests that other aspects of quality, such as improving academic achievement, can be addressed through the attainment of access, inclusion and equity. In focusing on basic values it suggests that focus on these aspects will also impact on the breadth and depth of the value of education for a child's personal, social and individual development.

4.2.8. The Review draws upon an inputs and outputs framework in discussing the classifying indicators of quality. This framework comprises four components a) Context; b) Inputs; c) Processes; d) Outputs and Outcomes. It suggests that for a deeper understanding of educational system performance a more analytical framework will be required. Priority issues affecting quality education are identified within the aforementioned four components and the requirements and relative cost of addressing the issues affecting quality is also discussed in the report.

4.2.9. The Review, the Monitoring Learning Achievement (MLA) test undertaken by UNRWA in 2009, and anecdotal evidence, all suggest that the current education system emphasises rote learning and memorisation, rather than the acquisition of skills and the development of understanding in terms of higher order cognitive abilities and their application. The Review, therefore, talks of the need to consider research which links classroom processes to the acquisition of higher order cognitive skills. It describes the difficulty of education often being subject to ⊠fads⊠ in curriculum, many of which are unproven in their relationship to outcomes. We would like to take this observation further and suggest that the rhetoric of terms such as `child centred' and `active learning' are seemingly not reflected in an understanding of what this means for day-to-day classroom practices, teaching style and methodology and what the implications for systemic support are, from the school to the policy development level. The challenge that UNRWA will face in implementing a reform which is based on practices that the key implementers, i.e. teachers and educational staff, have not experienced themselves should not be underestimated. Later in the description of the reform this challenge is linked directly to the rationale for using Open and Distance Learning (ODL) to train and professionally develop teachers.

4.2.10. A further difficulty in applying practices which encourage children to talk, question, think, hypothesise, investigate and evaluate, is that teachers already feel burdened by what is generally perceived as an excessive amount of subject content. Teacher training will need to emphasise new ways of interacting with "content". That is through an emphasis on skills development and understanding and the coverage of content to be integrated into this.

4.2.11. The Review discussion of quality education and reference to international definitions in determining and measuring quality education is reflected in the UNRWA Reform Strategy. Here, the broader definition of quality is adopted, learning is seen as more than memorisation of knowledge, teaching as more than transfer of content and schools as more than a place where this knowledge transfer takes place. Quality education is thus defined more in line with the Capability Approach (Chapter 2). The emphasis here is on the development of a child's potential in the broadest sense of human development. The classroom will thus be seen as a place to question, challenge, experiment and collaborate and the school as a safe and stimulating centre of excellence and community participation.

4.2.12. The Review describes Fields seeking to address identified learning problems by `doing more of what is not working' as one consequence of a lack of active learning models. It cites that this is the case even in Fields where there is a strong willingness to try new things, and discusses how these `more of the same' approaches, `involve more traditional teaching to students who have not succeeded with that model' (Quality in Education, p33).

4.2.13. In order to achieve a broader vision of quality, in line with both the observations and recommendations of the Review and the Capability Approach, the need for an overall strategy, led by the Education Department but developed in close collaboration with Fields and other stakeholders is clear. The Review emphasises that quick fixes may solve an immediate problem, but may complicate the quest for long-term quality at large. The present reform is thus based on this premise and what is known about change processes, and educational change most specifically.

4.3. Organisation and Management of UNRWA Education

4.3.1. This Organisation and Management Review Report begins by discussing the influence of external political, economic, social and cultural factors as related to education and the role of the Agency. It also discusses issues relating to:

1. Physical safety, which negatively affects the performance of students and teachers;
2. Restrictions on mobility, which have a direct impact on the provision of resources and accessibility of educational institutions;
3. High levels of unemployment in the region, which have significant consequences with regard to any restructuring scenarios;
4. Inability to set curriculum and political criticism of its content;
5. The high value placed on education by Palestinians;
6. UNRWA's obligation as a UN agency to ascribe to international objectives;
7. Challenges relating structures within UNRWA as related to OD and differences between international and local staff in the education programme and;
8. Non-systematic reporting of the monitoring of the education programme in medium term plans and the role of the ED.

Organisational Design of HQ

4.3.2. The Review identifies the key role that the Education Department at HQ has to play, within the overall organisation structure, but notes multiple competing demands from internal stakeholders and mixed impressions of the performance of the Department. The latter, it suggests, is based to a large extent on the number of staff in the department rather than their productivity, and cites how none of the critiques drew on a comparator, or any criteria related to efficiency (relating to inputs and outcomes/outputs).

4.3.3. One central problem which the Review highlights, in relation to roles, responsibilities and the strategic role of the Education Department, is the lack of analysis driving policy choices, with decisions made having negative impacts on resource efficiency. Similarly, it talks of a lack of a process for analysing the effectiveness and efficiency of education initiatives. Both areas are identified as having implications for a key role of the Education Department, particularly in the context of `shrinking resources and a desire for the highest quality results'.

4.3.4. At the heart of the Review's discussion around the organisation and management of the education programme lies the relatively recent decentralisation of service delivery. The Review highlights how the assumption made in the OD is that decentralizing education to the Fields will improve the effectiveness and efficiency of the Education Programme. It describes how decentralization seeks to "redistribute authority, responsibility, and financial resources for providing public services among different levels of organization." It suggests, however, that for this to be so, significant changes and capacity building will be required throughout the whole education system. In the short and medium-term, the Review points out that capacity building is expensive. The need for capacity development to support decentralisation is acknowledged, without strong initial input into systematic capacity development the process of decentralization can, as the Review points out, actually lead to results opposite to those planned. In the case of education this would mean increasing inequity and decreasing quality of provision, with a loss of overall agency coherence and policy frameworks, leading to fragmentation and low achievement. As the Review indicates, decentralised systems rely less on command and more on collaboration, but here it is important to note that for effective collaboration roles and responsibilities must be clearly defined, with all actors striving towards a shared vision, balancing the strategic with the contextual. In this regard, the shared vision should clearly relate to what is meant by quality education for Palestine refugees. Yet the Review sees both the Education Department and the Fields as having a relatively limited view of "a quality education, rather than one which will facilitate the acquisition of knowledge, skills, attitudes and values that will allow children to function effectively in society."

4.3.5. Following the development of a shared vision of quality education, a strategic direction must be determined towards its achievement. The Review cites the monitoring of this strategy as perhaps one of the most important aspects of the strategic change process that UNRWA is embarking upon. It describes how monitoring attempts to assess the alignment between what is planned for and what is being achieved. When properly thought through, it provides appropriate information to managers to work towards intended results. As the Review notes, `management for results' is a term used in the UN generally, and UNRWA more specifically, to highlight the importance managers place on attempting to understand how their plans are transformed into results. Using monitoring data to determine the extent to which fields and the ED are progressing towards meeting their strategic objective is necessary for engaging in strategic leadership and influencing change.

4.3.6. Strategic direction based on a shared vision thus needs to be supported by strong overall frameworks and substantiated by policies and plans. The Review notes that the current education governance framework does not clearly articulate the authority various actors have in making necessary decisions to guide components of the education system. It highlights how there is no visibly coherent framework that orders these directives and describes how typically, policy frameworks would include guidance on school operations, finance-budgets, school calendars, curriculum, student behaviour, teacher entry, evaluations, and so forth.

4.3.7. The UNRWA education programme operates within the broader frameworks of the UN practices and ethics, as well as the UNRWA interpretation of this at operational levels, with regard to Human Resource Management, Procurement, etc. For education, as the Review describes, there is a set of directives that touch on some of these areas but which are not complete, and no one holds a complete picture of the formal written governing documents. As a result, a great deal of the system governance occurs through the personal channels used by individual actors in the system. This, the Review observes, has proved particularly challenging since decentralisation, with confusion as to who does what. It notes that a reliance on HQ for more administrative tasks, such as the setting and marking of tests for recruitment, can be seen, although these administrative tasks would be clearly more meaningfully carried out at Field level, with the HQ focusing on ensuring that standards and norms, policies and frameworks are in place and monitoring adherence to them.

Partnerships

4.3.8. The Review discusses partnerships as contributing to organizational operations and effectiveness. UNRWA is currently developing an agency wide Partnership Policy. The value of partnerships is widely accepted, both as a key development tool, focusing on harmonisation, shared frameworks and responsibilities and, at institutional or organisational level, increasing the effectiveness of daily operations. More broadly, partnership offers a range of benefits, including exchanging approaches, keeping up with advances in related fields, gaining access to resources such as knowledge and expertise, and supporting joint work and collaboration.

4.3.9. The Review discusses how partnerships can take many forms and may be formal (for example, contractual agreements or MOUs) or informal. Partnering organisations might include institutions, organisations, groups or networks, collegial bodies, key constituents, and others. It highlights the cooperation and coordination links established over the years with a variety of bodies such as the ministries of education in the host countries and the Palestinian Authority, UNESCO, UNDP, UNICEF, WHO, and the League of Arab States. In addition, the Education Department works with local and international non-governmental organisations (NGOs) and Community Based Organisations (CBOs) within the five Fields.

4.3.10. The Review acknowledges the partnerships between the fields and other organisations but emphasises a need to strengthen and formalise these relationships. The UNRWA emerging Partnership Policy seeks to do precisely that, developing frameworks and structures to ensure partnership is beneficial to partners but, ultimately and above all, to the beneficiaries, the Palestine refugees. As part of the structural changes of the Education HQ, the Department has established a Partnership, Communication and ICT (PACICT) Unit, which is discussed in more detail in Chapter 5.

4.3.11. The Review places particular emphasis on the need to strengthen partnerships with host countries, seeing this as key to ensuring all Palestine refugee children obtain the basic knowledge and skills they need to have a high quality of life. The Review notes that these key relationships are not strategically articulated in either the FIPs or the HIP, and that the Education Department does not seem to play a role in building these critical partnerships. Rather relationships are Field based, with varying degrees of collaboration. The Review concludes by emphasizing that it is in the interest of the Education programme to strengthen these relationships and suggests that HQ Education Department should focus on strategic engagements and, together with Fields, build stronger partnerships with all host country ministries within which UNRWA schools operate.

4.3.12. Partnership should extend beyond the host countries and external agencies. Central to UNRWA's success as a service provider is the partnership between the fields and the HQ as discussed, but also between departments at the HQ. UNRWA is striving towards working more collaboratively as one agency and education must develop proactive and reactive relationships with all other departments, most specifically other programmatic departments, Human Resources, PCSU, Finance, Administration and External Relations and Public Information.

4.3.13. The importance of partnership in the delivery of a quality, efficient, and effective UNRWA education programme is reflected by the emphasis placed on it within the Education Reform Strategy. Here Partnership and Communication is one of the eight core reform programmes which is strengthened, as highlighted above, by the establishment of the PACICT Unit at HQ.

Programme management and processes

4.3.14. A discussion of the current EMIS suggests that the data is robust in some areas and deficient in others. The fact that two universal education indicators, GER and NER and survival rates are not addressed is highlighted. The Review also discusses the limited analysis which appears to take place in relation to the kind of statistics which are required by managers in order to analyse policy and improve the quality of education. The importance of relevant data, which is duly analysed and forms the basis of policy and decision making, was further emphasised by a research consultant, funded by Irish Aid, who undertook a short visit in September, 2010. He highlighted how too much data is collected, yet not enough is analysed.

Gender

4.3.15. Gender mainstreaming is an Agency priority and the Review suggests that whilst initial analysis showed that some progress has been made, many outputs have not yet been achieved. There are currently many opportunities for women in the UNRWA teaching profession, however, there is a need to achieve gender balance within the Education Faculties and at management level.

Human resources

4.3.16. Human Resource Management is substantively discussed and the Review notes a lack of human resource planning with regard to the education labour force. It talks of the importance of performance management and the role of incentives in motivating staff to do their best work in a challenging environment. For education, this highlights the need to develop core competencies and performance expectations for all cadres. The Review describes how these should relate to three broad areas of responsibility: professional, educational and management. The system developed by HR in collaboration with education staff in GFO and Education HQ, reflects the five overall categories of UNRWA—Service Delivery, Knowledge and Understanding, Attitude and Integrity, Relationships and Communication, Leadership and Management. The Education Department is now working closely with HR to develop interrelated competences for the support cadres, from the Head teacher to the Field Office.

4.3.17. More broadly with regard to Human Resources the Review specifies the need to :

1. Restructure the HQ Education Department;
2. Clarify the division of roles and responsibilities between HQ and Fields to reflect HQ's responsibility for strategy, policy, planning, standards, system performance, technical advising, external relations and the Field's responsibility for planning, implementing and monitoring the quality of education, teachers and schools, and collaborating with HQ and other fields;
3. Restructure the Education Programme in the Fields into a decentralised structure

4.3.18. The Education Reform Strategy is striving to achieve this clarity (see Chapter 5) and also provides a vehicle for the wider Sustaining Change agency agenda, which stresses the overall need to clarify the roles of HQ and fields and to better empower the Programmes in order that they provide strategic direction and appropriate support to the Fields. The importance of a not too tight, not too loose (Fullan, 2009) change process will guide the implementation of the Reform. There is a need for greater coherence in terms of a clear model of school support, with the appropriate development of capacity across the Agency, but fields must be able to make decisions based on their own context, as to how best to deploy their technical and financial resources to maximise their impact.

4.4. Evolving Nature of UNRWA Schools

4.4.1. In the "Evolving nature of UNRWA schools", the focus is on three elements of UNRWA schools:

1. The physical environment;
2. Teaching and learning; and
3. The student environment and student support systems.

4.4.2. Reference is made to the `School Improvement Framework' of the Australian Capital Territory of 2004, `The Constant Factors in Schooling' which states:

`The core business of schools is student learning and achievement. All school activity seeks to maximise learning outcomes for students. This includes all

dimensions of learning—academic, social, emotional, cultural and environmental.

The extent to which students are able to achieve their potential in terms of learning outcomes is, to some extent, dependent upon the capacity of the school to provide optimum learning circumstances for all students. High performing schools support student learning through best practice across a range of elements within the four domains of schooling:

- *Learning and teaching*
- *Student environment*
- *Leadership and management*
- *Community involvement*

`These four domains have been identified as the constant factors in schooling'.

4.4.3. The Review discusses each of these domains. With regard to the Physical Environment, the Review highlights UNRWA school infrastructure, overcrowded classrooms and double shift systems, and describing the negative impact they likely have on both the quality of the teaching and learning and student well being. In discussing Teaching and Learning the Review emphasises the importance of student-centred, activity based learning, but talks of how its achievement, across UNRWA, is constrained by an emphasis on traditional `high-stakes' examinations and the links to host country curriculum which focus on factual content and memorization. UNRWA's current examination system is seen to reflect the examination cultures of the host countries and the MENA area, yet the Review states that as such it is not best serving the UNRWA students. Rather, it is `driving instruction in ways that ignore the learning needs of students, and it is creating unnecessary stress for students and families'.

4.4.4. The Review further notes that in addition to these constraints, the current exam system is also based on the premise that the tests and the testing are valid. The Review suggests that even within what would be considered an educationally limited model of testing, the current approach is of questionable validity and that this is a key area for research that UNRWA should explore. The Review stresses that the obligation to meet the learning needs of students must be greater than the "obligation" to follow the host country curricula. It advocates for increased focus on numeracy and literacy skills, particularly in the early grades, with an overall emphasis on child-centred, activity-based learning at all grades and across all subjects.

4.4.5. The concerns outlined above notwithstanding, the Review also recognises that although those working to deliver UNRWA's Education Programme refer to multiple dimensions of education quality, `the pre-eminent concern of UNRWA and many of its Palestine refugee stakeholders is academic achievement, narrowly defined in terms of results on high stakes examinations, and benchmarked against available host government pass rates on state examinations'. As the Review states, the high value many Palestinians place on more traditional measures of high achievement influences UNRWA's struggle to deal with quality education. In the reminder that `just as health is more than prescriptions for drugs, education needs to be broader than student achievement in core subjects' lies a challenge for those responsible for the design and development of the UNRWA education reform. The engagement of a wide range of stakeholders in bringing about change in educational practice is thus likely to be imperative as UNRWA moves forward.

4.4.6. Such educational change cannot be brought about by a number of single innovations, but rather the whole education system must be addressed, from the way in which the teacher is taught, the functioning of the model of school education, the role of the school within the community, to an ethos of professional support and partnership, rather than one of supervision. Fullan highlights here how experience of reform supports an argument for systematic change, rather than a number of single innovations (Fullan, 2007).

4.4.7. The Review also highlights the difference that adopting a generalist class teacher model beyond lower elementary grades would make, both in terms of overall classroom ethos, and in terms of class size - the latter being significantly reduced. It describes how UNRWA schools have a wealth of specialist teachers, but suggests that the specialist teacher model results in much larger average class sizes than would be the case with generalist class teachers. Changing from a specialist to generalist model from classes 4-6 would also pave the way for greater interaction between pupils, teachers and parents and would support ongoing formative assessment of children, in order to provide them with additional support as and when required. The Review is also critical of grade repetition, referring to research that indicates that repeating a grade does not necessarily lead to academic improvement, and can create significant social and behavioural problems.

4.4.8. With reference to the third domain `The student environment and student support systems', the importance of employing a holistic approach to education - particularly when many Palestine refugee children live in conditions of immense stress - is discussed. Children living in such contexts need a school where they can express themselves, enjoy learning, learn social and life skills, and feel safe. A narrowly focused education system may, as the Review suggests, be conducive to violence in schools, such as bullying, fighting and harassment. The Review notes that human rights education is implemented across the Agency, although not necessarily consistently between schools and within classrooms. The Education Reform +seeks to address the consistency and quality of human rights education, not only as a key curriculum area, but also in terms of the more open, teaching and learning practices it encourages.

4.4.9. There is also discussion as to the roles of the educational cadre with respect to issues of school quality. This issue is also discussed in more depth in other sections of the Review, and at this stage it suffices to say that assistance to the educational support cadres, from School Supervisor to Area Education Officer and the Education Development Centre, will be central to the education reform.

4.5. Assessment of Teacher Education

4.5.1. The Review looks substantively at the provision of teacher education within UNRWA. The outstanding efforts and dedication of UNRWA teachers of the last 60 years is, as the Review reports, widely acknowledged. Similarly, the achievement, led by the Institute of Education (IE), in terms of laying the infrastructure for providing pre-and-in-service training has been a driving force in delivering teacher education over the years, is acknowledged. In the 1960s a joint Institute of Education was set up by UNRWA and UNESCO to train untrained teachers for the Palestine refugee students. The programme was mainly delivered through a model of distance learning courses, covering academic subject matter, and teacher methods. Teachers completed written assignments and there were weekly seminars. Perraton describes the programme as `successful in reducing the proportion of untrained teachers from 90% to 9% within five years'. He also describes the UNRWA/UNESCO programme as an exemplar for distance learning projects in southern Africa, although international legitimacy of this mode of delivery came in 1969 with the British Open University.

4.5.2. The way in which teacher education began in the UNRWA/UNESCO Institute of Education is particularly pertinent to the Education Reform Strategy and this is discussed more substantively in Chapter 5. However, it is important at this stage to note that the current methodology of the IE is described in the Review as a cascade model of training which:

1. Emphasises quantity over quality;
2. Is inefficient because of the separation between Headquarters and the Fields;
3. Loses efficiency because of the specialist focus of teachers;
4. Is costly in time and human resources relative to its quality.

4.5.3. The Review describes how the majority of UNRWA teachers begin their professional role without adequate pre-service preparation. It further observes that new teachers rely on `an obsolete training model which does not provide sufficient development and support, locking them into a teaching style reflecting how they (i.e., the teachers) were taught in school' as opposed to offering a more `holistic view of children's active learning or preparing them for the role they should undertake as a member of a school team working together to achieve school improvement'. It is further critical of the fact that there is no effective centralised monitoring and evaluation function within the IE, adding that there is neither a `framework with objectives, indicators of success, nor any coherent means of monitoring the performance of the in-service training system across Fields'.

4.5.4. With regards to the number of teachers trained, the Review highlights how the demand for teachers in UNRWA is approximately 1,500 per year, yet the supply of those who have had full training before entering the profession by UNRWA (from the Education Science Faculties) is around 380. As the Review points out, not all 380 will be able or want to pursue employment with UNRWA and the Review also highlights how UNRWA itself does not give these graduates preference. The Review describes how UNRWA `invests in a process to select the best of available candidates willing to work, this manifests itself in an elaborate screening process driven by examinations and a series of interviews. There is an over-supply of teachers in some areas, but the under-supply in some key areas has an overall adverse impact on the quality of teachers available to deliver quality education'.

4.5.5. The Review similarly highlights the need to provide ongoing professional support to teachers from the newly qualified stage, through their careers to become Headteachers, or other support cadres. Here, the Review suggests that UNRWA lacks an overall vision for teacher education, noting that in-service training has not changed in over 60 years and that the need to train large numbers from `scratch' has largely passed.

4.5.6. Reference is made to a World Bank study on education in the Arab World (2008) which links successful future reform to incentives and public accountability. One limitation of the UNRWA in-service training programme, highlighted by the Review, is that teacher education is not linked to career progression incentives as in UNRWA there is only one level of teacher. It describes how the current IE system focuses on new roles rather than accepted international concepts which see professional development taking place throughout a teacher's career. The focus on the provision of technical training of individual staff for the specialist roles that have traditionally formed the basis of UNRWA's current establishment is noted. The Review describes this training as unlikely to be ongoing and is of shorter duration than suggested in international norms.

4.5.7. Overall, the Review emphasises that current teacher courses make little use of competency approaches which focus on professionalisation, teamwork and peer learning. Further, it states that the traditional approach adopted does not incorporate best practice international standards to effect positive change in schools. It suggests that current training is not geared to supporting the new requirements of the Organizational Development process, or the priorities of Field Implement Plans (FIPs), such as support for school improvement, schools of excellence, or career-long professional development.

4.5.8. To achieve UNRWA's vision, as implied in the OD process, there is an implicit demand for in-service training to move away from functional specialisation to focusing on soft skills, such as problem solving, teamwork, change management and communication. However, there is no explicit articulated demand for such approaches. This lack of demand is not surprising, and neither are the Review findings showing a level of trainee satisfaction with the IE programme, although this varies between levels and across fields. Teachers are likely to appreciate professional development of any sort, and there is no question that those delivering training have subject and professional expertise.

However, teachers and their trainers may not know of a wider range options or alternatives in order to fully evaluate the relative merits of what they are currently being offered.

4.5.9. The Institute of Education still plays a central role in the provision of traditional courses, those for new untrained teachers, Headteachers and Supervisors. The Review highlights however that Field Offices have responded to local needs, seeking support from other providers, in partnership with development partners, and running their own teacher training programmes. As there is no overall UNRWA mechanism for quality control of these courses, and no shared vision of quality education, it is likely that they are addressing a perceived immediate need. Although courses may have some impact, this is likely to be limited, as the education system as a whole will not have been reconfigured to support new approaches. It also has undoubtedly led to fragmentation of the UNRWA education programme, and is moving UNRWA away from a coherent model of pre-service and life long teacher professional development to one of fragmented provision.

4.5.10. The Education Reform, discussed in Chapter 5, places teacher education at its heart, and suggests that in working with teachers and other stakeholders, the Education Department should take a lead role, drawing on international best practices and research to develop relevant and up to date programmes and delivery modes for UNRWA teachers. The vision for teacher education reflects the recommendations of the Review, particularly with regards to differentiated levels of teachers linked to professional development and performance evaluation. The specialist model of teacher training is described as suited to a specialist conception that UNRWA has followed to date, but as limiting flexibility and making little use of contemporary knowledge. This approach is limiting the model of teaching and learning with the current practice supporting neither the holistic education that UNRWA advocates for, nor a model of teacher training and ongoing professional development that the Agency would strive to establish. Already Fields are considering implementing a generalist model for Grade 4. The Headquarters must therefore support a full scale study into the feasibility and implications of an overall UNRWA move away from specialist teaching in the `primary' years.

4.5.11. The Review reports the lessons highlighted by World Bank studies from developed countries, noting that "policy experience of OECD countries on teacher education highlights the need to: a) shift to focus from individual abilities to communities of practice and to development of teacher capacities; b) recognise school culture as an asset not an obstacle; c) link teacher development with leadership development and d) treat teacher education as a career long development process".

4.5.12. Highlights of the Review recommendations in the area of teacher education are:

1. New role for Headquarters in teacher education

2. New role for IE which is less operational and more strategic/framework oriented
3. Field offices to explore relationships with host country institutions and shared use of ESFs

4.5.13. In the 1960s UNRWA moved from 90% to 9% of teachers being untrained, and today there are approximately 2,000 who have not gone through in-service training yet. Only a small percentage of teachers who are recruited to UNRWA schools have any pre-service training. Traditionally apart from the graduates of the ESFs all teachers are trained in-situ through the Institute of Education inservice Education Psychology programme. UNRWA surprisingly has moved away from the use of distance learning—which it deployed in the 1960s—for the training of its teachers. Since 2006 UNRWA Policy mandates that teaching is a degree profession. To-date there are around 1,700 teachers without a university degree.

4.5.14. Internationally the use of open and distance or blended learning has gained credibility in both developed and developing contexts with much experience of it being specifically, successfully deployed for teacher education. The Universalia Review does not discuss the role of using a blended (multi-media) approach to Open and Distance Learning (ODL) for UNWRA teachers. However, the recommendations it makes with regard to modern approaches to training, support materials, greater networking of teachers and teacher educators, and training located closer to the schools, are consistent with deploying an ODL approach. The use of ODL can achieve much in terms of quality provision, training of support cadres, and economies of scale and is discussed more fully in Chapter 5 in the context of the Education Reform.

4.6. Special Education Programming

4.6.1. The Review's report on Special Education references the UNESCO EFA Global Monitoring Report for 2008 and the estimate that, worldwide, 3% of primary age children have intellectual, physical, hearing or visual impairments. The GMR further states that many more children, however, have mild to moderate learning disabilities and that in many developed countries these children are included in statistics on disabilities and in estimates of special education needs, and can make up a very large percentage of children receiving special education services. However, in many developing countries, where systems for the assessment and diagnosis of learning disabilities have not been developed, these children might never be identified as having a learning disability, might drop out in primary grades, or may never have attended school at all. UNESCO concludes that, particularly in developing countries "children with disabilities have to combat blatant educational exclusion".

4.6.2. The Review sees the development of comprehensive SEN programming, with access for all special needs children to appropriate, quality education, as a major undertaking for UNRWA. It describes such an endeavour as one which will require strong leadership at the Headquarters, Field, Area and School levels to create an environment of acceptance of and respect for, SEN children, and to encourage collaboration, support and accountability across the system. While this is a huge task, the right of all Palestine refugee children, including disabled children, to an education is a basic human right, a right to which UNRWA, the United Nations and donors have all made a strong commitment.

4.6.3. The Review suggests that the development of SEN programming will have `tremendous financial implications' and that advocacy on behalf of UNRWA SEN children with donors will be critical. It states that the development of sound SEN programming also has implications for the Middle East region; SEN systems in host countries are still developing and UNRWA can potentially take a much-needed leadership position in this area.

4.6.4. A summary of the recommendations made by the Review reports which UNRWA supports follows:

1. Special Education Needs Taskforce to be established with representation from FOs, HQ (including Health and RSS Departments) and other stakeholders;
2. SEN policy, framework and M&E to be developed;
3. SEN partnerships with a range of organizations and host countries to be established;
4. Policy development to be supported with outside technical expertise. A range of pre and in-service teacher training programmes to be developed.

4.6.5. The UNRWA Education Reform articulates special needs more broadly as Inclusive Education, reflecting the global discourse and development of thinking and practices in this field. The emphasis placed on Inclusive Education is reflected in both its centrality in the reform programme, discussed in Chapter 5, and in the restructuring of the `Headquarters' Education Department, where the responsibility for strategic direction and support to Inclusive Education across UNRWA lies with a Unit with the same title.

4.7. Response to the Universalia Review

4.7.1. It is recognised that the Universalia Review provides a highly comprehensive assessment of many of the key elements of the UNRWA education programme. Our response is one of strong agreement with the overall analysis of the UNRWA education programme. That is: the expressed fundamental need to change classroom practices; to move from what is perceived as a fragmented approach to achieving quality to one of greater strategic coherence; to ensure relevant and effective pre-service and life long training of teachers; to clarify and strengthen organisational roles and responsibilities relationship both between the Fields and the HQ, and within the Fields and to place greater emphasis on partnerships.

4.7.2. Issues of education quality within UNRWA were comprehensively addressed throughout the Review and reference made to global practices, educational research, knowledge and understanding. Some areas, important to the overall strategic analysis, were not substantively addressed, and these include: (i) an analysis of the external (operating) environment and (ii) a review of the financial resources available to

UNRWA and the trends and challenges involved (Yates, 2010). To this effect a complementary comprehensive analysis of the external environment, with regard to regional, social, economic, cultural, technological and educational factors was undertaken (Chapter 2).

4.7.3. Similarly some technical areas, such as work in the areas of Quality Assurance and ICTs, were not fully addressed in the Review. It is also noted that the Review team were not mandated to cover UNRWA's provision of TVET. The Education Reform Strategy thus seeks to address these areas. With regard to TVET the Reform emphasises its provision as a key option for students' education, and one which can help address issues of unemployment, underdevelopment and contribute to overall stability.

4.7.4. This Education Reform Strategy directly addresses the need, articulated in the Review, for the HQ to provide strategic direction, in order to move the UNRWA Education Programme away from being `a system which has not sufficiently evolved to current education best practices' to one which is responsive to the needs of the Palestine refugee systems in the 21st century. Similarly the opportunities to `do more with the resources at hand', as well as to do more with `more resources' is duly noted.

4.7.5. As the Universalia Review did not conceptualise the Reform as a whole, or seek to prioritise key interventions, it served as a spring board for an inclusive UNRWA wide process of development for the Education Reform Strategy.

Chapter 5

The Reform

5.1. Overview

5.1.1. A strategic approach to education reform is crucially important for the future well being of the Palestinian people. In many ways the realisation of the future hopes, aspirations and the continued visibility of the Palestinian cause rest on the effectiveness of UNRWA's, and ultimately the Palestine, education system (Yates, 2010).

5.1.2. Any reform must take into account what is known about school effectiveness, particularly with regard to the emphasis placed on the teacher and Headteacher. It must acknowledge the existing system and the context in which the system operates. For UNRWA, the context of refugees living in five Fields, awaiting a resolution to a 60 year old problem, with education service provision being the responsibility of a UN agency, but following the curriculum of the host country, combined with the additional layer of political perceptions and sensitivities, is one which is particularly challenging.

5.1.3. The Reform therefore must place itself within this context, as well as consider UNRWA's organisational structural implications of decentralization in order to implement a change that is in alignment. Similarly, it is not the time to consider any dismantling of the current education system and structure, but it is instead time to strengthen and increase the effectiveness of that which is already in place. It is important to note here, however, that although existing systems will be deployed, this is not in contradiction to the systemic change required in order to get UNRWA's education programme back on track and relevant to the current and future needs of Palestine refugees.

5.1.4. Systemic change in this instance means addressing all elements of the system in a coherent and cohesive way. UNRWA's Education Reform will seek to change classroom practice, that is the way in which teachers teach and children are given the opportunity to learn. It will promote an ethos of the schooling which supports a holistic view of learning for all children, with strong links between the school parents and the local community. It will further seek to ensure that the professional and administrative support structures in the field work together more cohesively to address and support the required changes.

5.1.5. The Reform will also work to ensure that all educational structures and systems, from the school to the Headquarters, operate within a strengthened overall environment as reflected in UNRWA wide policies and strategies. These frameworks will be developed and designed in alignment with those existing or emerging at an Agency wide level. Of particular significance here will be those relating to Human Resource development, governance, and ethical behaviour.

5.2. Reform concept and rationale

5.2.1. As the analysis of the socio-economic political context of the regional and specifically of the UNRWA education programme highlighted, there are a range of challenges in the region. Some of these have impact on the UNRWA education programme in addition to the specific challenges of access, relevance and equity. The education programme must address the needs of the most vulnerable, and as such will be in line with the Agency's Poverty Policy. Similarly the need to ensure gender equity and empowerment of both girls and boys, women and men to achieve their potential, whether as students or as UNRWA educational staff must underpin the design and development of any reform strategy.

5.2.2. Within host countries, there is a growing recognition of the need for improvement in the area of education, as reflected by the UNESCO EFA Global Monitoring Report and other regional reports and studies. If the region is to realise fully its EFA targets education delivery must be reconceptualised, in terms of the inputs, processes and outcomes. The current regional model of education can be seen to impose some constraints on the UNRWA education programme, most specifically with the adherence to host country curriculum—often described as overloaded and exam-oriented—and the resultant teaching methodology and ethos of schooling.

5.2.3. An UNRWA Education Reform Strategy which focuses on a more current and relevant approach to education can enable it to contribute positively to the educational discourse and practices taking place across the region. UNRWA could once again be in the driving seat, in terms of educational practices, and this will serve to strengthen the partnership and relationship with the host countries. The education Reviews and the `Light Touch' Organisational Development review, and the subsequent emerging Sustaining Change Reform Strategy all highlight the need to bring strategic coherence back to programme delivery. As Fullan points out, strategic coherence and contextualisation are not contradictory (Fullan, 2007), rather contextual factors should be addressed within Agency-wide policy frameworks, standards and norms.

5.2.4. It is crucial to build capacity at all levels to ensure shared understanding and commitment to a vision of quality education at systemic, institutional/ organizational and individual levels. The Reform Strategy will seek to address all three levels in an interrelated way, with roles and responsibilities clearly defined and, appropriate support given to facilitate effective performance within those roles. In order to achieve this, and as discussed throughout, agency level frameworks, decision making bodies and accountability mechanisms are required. This will support an Agency-wide implementation of decentralisation, as expressed in the OD review, that is decentralisation where there is an agreed balance between Agency-wide and Field specific operational contextualisation.

5.2.5. The process of developing this Reform Strategy thus reflects the key principles of change management processes. In the context of lessons learned from OD, principally for a shared understanding of the need for change and a consistent, explicit statement of a future vision and ongoing communication with all stakeholders. For refugees and host governments this vision should be conveyed in a clear statement on the provision of services and assurance of quality. For staff and managers, it will relate also to what is expected from them and how the organization will support them in the realization of these expectations. Funding agencies and donors will require an understanding of how resources will be utilised to improve services (new and existing), secure efficiencies and lever in other finance. They also need to be able to identify their return on investment[2] and see UNRWA's contribution to the achievement of the MDGs and local and regional development.

5.2.6. Many examples of failed education reform can be found. As Fullan stresses, educational reform is about changing the culture and dynamics of classrooms, schools, districts/areas, managers and in this way it affects multiple levels. Evidence has shown how large scale reform is the most `promising', but that it should

[2] Quote from OD Keith Doran, consultant for Sustaining Change, October 2010

strive to be neither too tight, nor too loose, nor too top down, or too bottom up. Rather it should seek to harness the strengths of all stakeholders in a coherent, interrelated way, and build capacity with a focus on results. Reference is made to how large scale education reform has failed when it has focused primarily on the development of innovations or on accountability, without due attention to ownership or capacity development. To this effect the UNRWA Education Reform Strategy comprises eight (8) interrelated strands from governance frameworks, to teachers and their development, curriculum enrichment and support, inclusive education, with all aspects underpinned and supported by research and an effective Agency wide Education Management Information System.

5.2.7. For any transformational change, which is the aspiration in developing the Education Reform, it is essential that front line staff is actively engaged in the conceptualisation of the change and in the ensuing implementation process (Fullan, 2009). In this respect, UNRWA faces particular challenges with the differing perceptions, needs and values of the staff and the complexity of the environments they are accountable to—the refugee community of which they themselves are members, the host countries within which they live and work, and the UNRWA educational operational structures at Field level and HQ.

5.3. Reform beneficiaries

5.3.1. The beneficiaries of the UNRWA educational reform will be the learners participating in, and benefiting from, the UNRWA education programme.

Similarly, teachers are also primary beneficiaries as they are UNRWA's single most important educational resource[3]. The development of teacher's capacity and their professional empowerment is the heart of the educational Reform. Secondary beneficiaries will be those responsible for designing and implementing the Reform Strategy across the Agency such as Field-based school and teacher support cadres, Field managers and the Department of Education in headquarters. Ultimately, the Education Reform Strategy will contribute to the vision of UNRWA to serve Palestine refugees in order to achieve their full potential.

5.4. Reform strategic context

5.4.1. The Reform Strategy is consistent with the achievement of the global EFA goal, and is aligned with the educational aspirations of the region, as discussed in Chapter 2. The strategy is placed within the UNRWA Medium Term Strategy and its Biennium Plans and encapsulates the UNRWA planning objectives, outputs and outcomes in a coherent, strategic way. Similarly, the education change management process outlined herein embodies the principles of the OD, and as such could serve as a vehicle for strengthening OD across the agency. This would be achieved by clarifying the roles and responsibilities of HQ and Field, as discussed in OD, but in specific relation to the educational cadres and then building capacity accordingly. In this way lessons can be learned, models tried and tested, and interrelationships understood and this can be of value agency-wide.

---

[3] GMR, 2010

5.5. Reform objectives vision

5.5.1. The Education programme vision is aligned with the overall UNRWA Vision:

> *"For every Palestine refugee to enjoy the best possible standards of human development especially attaining his or her full potential individually and as a family and community member; being an active and productive participant in socio-economic and cultural life and feeling assured that his or her rights are being defended, protected and preserved". (Source: MTS: 2010:9)*

5.5.2. The focus of the Reform is on education as providing the means to achieving this overall vision, but with the concept of `human development' and `attainment of the full potential' reflecting more holistic values of a quality education system, that is:

> *An UNWRA education system which develops the full potential of Palestine refugees to enable them to be confident, innovative, questioning, thoughtful, tolerant and open minded, upholding human values and religious tolerance, proud of their Palestinian identity, and contributing positively to the development of their society and the global community. (Source: Quality Education Retreat March 2010, and Dead Sea Strategic Retreat Workshop June 2010)*

5.5.3. Education, as a means to realising greater human development and potential, is in line with the ideas expressed in the Capability Approach. At the heart of the CA lies the notions of capabilities, meaning an individual's freedom to realise beings and doings that they have reason to value (Unterhalter 2007; Alkire 2003, Sen 1999 etc) and wellbeing, often understood as a person's "effective opportunities to undertake the actions and activities that they want to engage in, and be whom they want to be" (Robeyns 2003:7). Sen (2001), the Nobel Laureate who developed the approach, argues that the focus of development should be on increasing wellbeing by removing the barriers that prevent people from realising and expanding their capabilities.

5.5.4. The Capability Approach, thus is a framework which allows consideration to what extent individuals have freedom to achieve that which they have reason to value (Robeyns 2005). It offers three clear advantages over traditional economic and quantitative output oriented models. Firstly, its emphasis on wellbeing, and its holistic understanding of what constitutes this; secondly, its valuing of agency and the ability of individuals to chose and exercise autonomy; and thirdly, its recognition of the importance of creating environments where each individual is able to convert their resources into valued functionings (Vaughan 2007). Gladwell (2009) argues that this way of thinking has profound implications for education policy and practice in protracted, urban refugee situations.

5.5.5. The Capability Approach would here suggest that the rights and entitlements of one group are no more important than another, and that individuals should be treated equally, regardless of whether or not they are within their own nation state. With particular regard to education, Nussbaum insists that institutions must use education to "enhance the lives of the poorest and the most neglected" (2005:217 in Gladwell 2009); a description very often applicable to UNRWA's population of concern.

5.5.6. The vision of the Reform is relevant also to the `highly complex, dynamic and inherently unstable situation [of Palestine refugees], with the key being to develop a system that builds energising and enabling frameworks which are responsive to the opportunities and that build on the strengths of the resources available and which also clearly match the specific circumstances of time and place' (Yates, 2010).

5.6. Reform description

5.6.1. Of the eight identified reform focus areas, there are four which are substantive, that is, programme focused, and four which are essential in ensuring that reform is successfully and sustainability implemented. Substantive programmes relating directly to service delivery are: Teacher Development and School Empowerment (TDSE), Inclusive Education, Curriculum and Student Assessment and Technical and Vocational Education and Training. These foci reflect what is known about the determinants of quality education, the Universalia education Review findings and recommendations, the priorities for education reform in host countries, and the remit for UNRWA's educational provision.

5.6.2. The Reform activities, towards achieving the Outputs, all reflect three core principles; (a) collaboration between Field offices and Headquarters with either taking a `substantive' lead role, (b) harnessing external expertise, and (c) emphasising partnerships with host governments and other stakeholders. The modalities of the reform will be strategic, policies, frameworks and also generic tools to assess students' needs, and high quality School Based Teacher Development material for training teachers and the professional support cadres.

5.7. Reform programmes

Overview

5.7.1. The four substantive Reform programmes are:

1. TeacherDevelopmentandSchoolEmpowerment;
2. Inclusive Education;
3. Technical and Vocational Training and Youth; and
4. Curriculum and Student Assessment.

The four support areas (i.e., supporting substantive reform programme delivery) are:

1. Research, Development and EMIS;
2. Governance;
3. Strategic Planning, Management and Projects; and
4. Partnerships, Communication and ICTs;

5.7.2. Each of the reform programmes was developed using a Logical Framework approach. The Reform Programme Logframes are available for reference in the

Annex 3 of this Strategy. The Reform Implementation Document (RID) provides a full narrative of the programmes including: Background, Rationale, Host Country operations, UNRWA current status, Challenges and Constraints and details of the Outputs, Activities, Costing, Monitoring and Evaluation. Below an overview of the eight programmes is provided.

Teacher Development and School Empowerment

5.7.3. Research has identified the teacher as the single most important education resource (2010 GMR). Top performing countries in education have invested in their teaching force, ensuring that they `get the best teacher; get the best out of them' and that teachers provide ongoing support to learners to ensure they do not lag behind (GMR, 2010). To this effect teachers are central to the Education Reform.

5.7.4. Over the last decades UNRWA, with the support of UNESCO, has achieved much with regard to the development of a teaching cadre. Since UNRWA began training teachers in 1964 it has trained more than 32,000 teachers. The current teacher training system however has capacity constraints, especially with regard to ongoing professional development with an average of 1,000 teachers, Headteachers and Supervisors out of approximately 18,000 within a calendar year.

5.7.5. The Universalia Review highlighted that the teaching model remains didactic, teacher-based and as such is unlikely to support the needs of the learners. Students' achievement in the 2009 MLA achievement tests do appear to substantiate this, with performance in core subject areas of Maths and Arabic in Grades 4 and 8, across all five Fields, consistently lower than anticipated. The difference in student performances was greater within a Field, than between the Fields and the performance of boys was noticeably lower than that of girls. The analysis of the findings also indicated that children particularly underperformed on higher order thinking—that is the application of rules to problem solving and more open ended tasks.

5.7.6. There is thus a need to revisit the way in which teachers are recruited, trained and supported. The Education Reform Strategy will therefore aim to improve the level of provision of teacher training and substantively modify pedagogic practices and delivery mechanisms. To this end it will support the development of an overall UNRWA Teacher Policy and Strategy, one which addresses issues from recruitment, training, and career progression to performance evaluation. Training of teachers will be intensified with emphasis placed on pre-service training, ongoing professional development, and monitoring and evaluation of the impact of training undergone.

5.7.7. Similarly, the capacity of the Headteacher and the school as a whole, through a model of school empowerment, will be strengthened. This will include the use of multi-media materials—from print to compute—to support the professional development of UNRWA teachers, Head-teachers and support cadres across the five fields of operation. Evidence shows that Open and Distance Learning (ODL) can be successfully deployed for all five components of teacher education:

general education, strengthening teachers' knowledge of the subjects they teach, teaching pedagogy, child development and towards the achievement of good classroom practices.

Outcome:	Professional, qualified and motivated teaching force and empowered schools in place
Outputs	
Outputs 1	Teacher policy and strategic implementation framework in place
Outputs 2	Coherent teacher training and professional development structures in place
Outputs 3	Effective management of teaching profession and administrative systems in place
Outputs 4	Status and working conditions of teachers enhanced
Outputs 5	A model of school empowerment developed and implemented

Output 1: A draft Policy prepared by a team from TDSE at HQ (A) will form the basis of work with Field colleagues, supported by a consultant with expertise in the area of teacher policies. HR and the Fields will be fully engaged in the process of policy development and implementation. The Policy will consider issues pertaining to teachers from recruitment criteria—moving away from an emphasis only on academic qualifications to consider skills, aptitudes and motivation—'to professional development and career progression of teachers. This will be in line with the Human Resource strategies for talent management, with opportunities for progression articulated through

levels and bands, which are in line with the emerging Compensation Framework. Policy simulations and projection tools will be developed and deployed in collaboration with the fields.

Output 2: The focus of teacher training will be on developing school based teacher development through the use of blended learning. International expertise will support UNRWA in the design and development of school based programmes with appropriate support and delivery systems. An Open and Distance Learning (ODL) Policy will reflect the way in which this modality will be used to support teacher development. The Policy will provide the rationale for this approach, specify target groups, discuss implementation modalities and address costing issues.

The School Based Teacher Development (SBTD) programme will enable teachers to learn in situ, reflect on their own ways of teaching, be exposed to international best practices and knowledge as to how children learn and the implications for teaching. The initial focus of the School Based Teacher Development (SBTD) programme will be Continuing Professional Development (CPD) of teachers. This approach will also be deployed for Headteachers, again drawing on international support in the area of school leadership and management training. Courses will later be deployed for Newly Qualified Teachers (NQTs). Through the school based approaches the professional development of support cadres (Supervisors, Area Education Officers etc) will be explicitly addressed. The target group of the first School Based Teacher

Development programme, as agreed by all Fields, is teachers of Grade 1 to 6. Here, the emphasis will be on enhancing teachers' understanding of effective teaching and learning practices.

Output 3: Achieving successful outcomes through ODL approaches is dependent on more than ensuring high quality, accessible and relevant training materials - although these are obviously crucial. It is also about administrative and professional support systems and structures, financing, budgeting and costing, student support, assessment and accreditation, management, administration and advocacy, quality assurance and monitoring and evaluation in ODL. To this end, with support from experts in these areas, a system of implementing the ODL programmes will be mapped out. This will build upon and strengthen existing Field education structures with training material produced Supervisors, Areas Officers and the Education Development Centres. A generic `Template' for implementing SBTD will guide Fields in determining the most appropriate implementation model for their context. There will be a much greater emphasis on these cadres mentoring and coaching teachers rather than `supervising' or cascading training.

Through the HR Performance Management Systems (PMS) these new approaches to classroom practice and provision of professional support to teachers will be further endorsed. All training and Continuing Professional Development (CPD) for educators will align with the Competencies required for their post, and the Performance Evaluation Reporting (PER) system will thus be a key to evaluation and career progression. In ensuring the PER system works effectively, close coordination with HR will be essential.

Output 4: Studies will be undertaken in order to explore the current status of teachers, and intrinsic and extrinsic factors which impact on their professional motivation. This will be in conjunction with the PA, UNESCO and ILO—building on ongoing similar studies. Findings will further support the development of the Teacher Policy. An Advocacy Strategy will be established to raise the status of teachers in the community in a number of ways, for example through Teacher Awards and World Teachers' Day celebrations.

Output 5: This output relates to empowerment of the school as a whole, and this will be complementary to the training and professional development of individual teachers or staff within the school. The SBTD programme will be a key contributory dimension to school empowerment School Quality Reviews will be carried out and the Department For International Development (DFID) supported `School as a Focus of Development Programme' will serve as a useful resource in this area.

Cross cutting issues

Gender, inclusive education and human rights are considered crucial cross cuttings dimensions of all teacher training programmes. To date the training programmes produced by the Institute of Education have sought to address gender and human rights specifically. It will be important to ensure that all cross cutting issues, including protection and UNRWA Protection Standards relevant to education, are fully integrated into the Teacher Policy and the new Open and Distance Learning programmes.

Partnerships

Strategic partnerships for the development of policies and high quality training programmes will be important. To this effect, for example, links have already been established - through the New York Liaison Office Partnership Forum—with institutions/organisations working in the area of teacher development across the MENA region. A plan for moving expressions of collaboration forward will be put in place.

Links with host governments

With regard to teacher issues, UNRWA is working closely with the Ministry of Education and Higher Education (MoEHE) of the Palestinian National Authority. The PA is currently implementing an EU funded, UNESCO supported programme, which looks at all aspects of teacher development from policy frameworks, status and conditions, initial training to ongoing professional development. The Reform also provides a platform to strengthen links with other host countries.

Programme management

The HQ Teacher Development and School Empowerment Unit is responsible for managing the overall reform programme in this area, working collaboratively with other Units in the Education Department HQ-most specifically Research and Development and EMIS; Partnership, Communication and ICTs; Curriculum Enrichment; Student Assessment; and Inclusive Education—and with the Fields. Ongoing collaboration with the Human Resources Department will also be crucial.

Monitoring and evaluation

This will be through the implementation of a Monitoring and Evaluation plan developed for the overall Education Reform Programme. There will be similarly need to be Monitoring and Evaluation mechanisms in place to address this specific reform area.

Inclusive Education

Overview

5.7.8. The principle of inclusion is that no group of any population is less able to access and benefit from services delivered. The Agency's work is governed by international human rights instruments and the principles of non-discrimination and protection of the integrity of the human being. UNRWA strives thus to explicitly ensure that certain groups, such as persons with disabilities or traumatised persons in conflict ridden and fragile environments, vulnerable and marginalised groups, or children and youth with special education needs do not face stigma and attitudinal, or other, barriers to participation. Currently there are an estimated 100,000 students in UNRWA institutions with Special Education Needs who are not being catered for. In line with UNRWA's vision, the goal of IE is to assure the rights of all refugee children - regardless of gender, abilities, disabilities, impairments, health conditions and socio-economic status-to equal access to a meaningful and quality education. To this effect an increased focus on the area of Inclusive Education is needed.

5.7.9. The first step towards more Inclusive Education will be to develop shared definitions of Special Education Needs (SEN) terminology. An Inclusive Education policy will be developed to provide guidelines for Fields to determine how best to support children with Special Education Needs. Capacity development for teachers in the area of psychosocial support will be of particular significance and Education will work closely with Health and Relief and Social Services in developing policies and support strategies.

Outcome:	Equal access for all children to quality education regardless of gender, abilities, disabilities, impairments, health conditions and socio-economic status assured.
Outputs	
Outputs 1	Inclusive Education Policy and framework in place
Outputs 2	Systems to identify and respond to diverse needs of children strengthened
Outputs 3	Gender equity enhanced
Outputs 4	Healthy school environment supported
Outputs 5	Psychosocial needs of children identified and addressed

Output 1: An Inclusive Education policy and framework based on a review of issues and current status of Inclusive Education and Special Education Needs practices across the Fields will be put in place. The development of the Inclusive Education policy and framework will involve technical support from international expert(s), interaction with the Field programme staff. To enhance understanding of Inclusive Education and importance of addressing the needs of all students, a range of communication and advocacy materials, such as leaflets, brochures and DVDs, will be developed in coordination with PIO.

Output 2: An effective system to identify and support all children with diverse needs enrolled in UNRWA schools will be established. This will require the development of tools and materials for the implementation of Inclusive Education practices. Capacity of teachers will also be developed through the School Based Teacher Development Programme (see Outcome 1) and other targeted training.

Output 3: In line with the PCSU led Gender Action Plan for education, the focus of this Output will be an analysis of existing curriculum material and teaching approaches with regard to gender equity. The UNRWA Gender Mainstreaming Strategy will also feed into the development of Teacher Gender Guidelines.

Output 4: Building on the strong collaboration between the Education and Health Department, a School Health Strategy will be developed. This will take into account current status issues and practices.

Output 5: The psychosocial impact of the Palestine refugee context can adversely affect the educational, personal and social development of UNRWA students. To this effect, a review of current literature (e.g. UNESCO, 2010 Psychosocial Assessment of Education in Gaza and Recommendations for Response) will form the basis for the development of a strategy to address needs. Teacher support materials will be produced and capacity developed accordingly.

Cross cutting issues

UNRWA strives to ensure that the key cross cutting issues of Gender, Youth, Disability, Environment and Protection are substantively addressed through its programme delivery. In line with the UNRWA Education Gender Strategy, Disability Strategy, UNRWA Protection Standards and the Education Technical Instructions and Guidelines related to Safe and Violence Free Schooling, and the emerging policies regarding Environment and Youth, the Inclusive Education programme will spearhead activities to ensure that quality educational delivery is safe, accessible and of relevance to all children.

Partnerships

The Inclusive Education programme will be planned and implemented in close partnership with international, regional and local agencies. Partnership with relevant UN agencies, such as UNESCO and UNICEF and other international agencies who work for women, youth, disabled, human rights, and environment, will be pursued and established. In this way UNRWA will draw upon existing norms, standards, guidelines and training and learning materials. Partnerships at local level with governmental and non-governmental organizations, institutions and hospitals and special schools will facilitate support in referral purposes and rehabilitation services for those children with more extreme needs. The success of the Inclusive Education programme will also depend on the close cooperation it maintains withinUNRWA, with the Department of Health, Department of Relief and Social Services and Department of Camp Development and infrastructure both at HQ and Field level.

Links with host governments

Strong relationships with local governments are key for the effective implementation of an Inclusive Education programme in UNRWA schools, in terms of shared expertise, capacity development of technical staff and access to support equipment and infrastructure. UNRWA, with its resource constraints, may not be able to have its own highly trained technical staff or the required infrastructure and equipment. To this effect there will be a need to establish close relationships with all agencies/councils in the Government responsible for different groups, such as the Disability council.

Programme management

The overall management of this programme will be under the Inclusive Education Unit, in coordination with Fields. Close collaboration will be needed with all Units in the Education Department.

Monitoring and Evaluation

This will be through implementation of a Monitoring and Evaluation plan developed for the overall Education Reform Programme. There will, similarly, need to be Monitoring and Evaluation mechanisms in place to address this specific reform focus area.

Technical and Vocational Education and Training (TVET) and Youth

Overview

5.7.10. The TVET reform programme will work to improve employability for Palestine refugee youth through market-responsive, quality Technical and Vocational Education and Training. To-date, more than 77,000 trainees have graduated from UNRWA's VTCs and a high employment rate of graduates has been achieved. However, current rates of supply cannot keep up with the increasing demand; in 2008/2009 for example only 30% of VTC applicants could be accommodated.

5.7.11. The TVET and Youth programme will support the Fields in reaching a larger number of students and in particular, targeting vulnerable youth, both male and female. The Reform will also seek to address the relevance and responsiveness of TVET programmes to labour market needs, as highlighted in the external analysis of UNRWA's operating context (Chapter 2). To this effect, new courses, both in terms of their focus and their delivery modality, will be designed; and there will be greater emphasis on the development of entrepreneurial skills.

5.7.12. To achieve its aim the TVET reform programme will also create placement and learning opportunities with industry, establish partnerships with a range of stakeholders, and put in place TVET agency-wide quality assurance management systems.

Outcome:	Relevant and quality Technical Vocational Education and Training (TVET) structures/ programmes in place
Outputs	
Outputs 1	Access to TVET particularly for vulnerable groups and youth enhanced
Outputs 2	Relevance and responsiveness of TVET programs to labour market needs strengthened
Outputs 3	TVET quality assurance system in place
Outputs 4	Sustainability of VTCs supported
Outputs 5	Effective guidance and placement system in place

Output 1: Enhancing access to UNRWA TVET, particularly for vulnerable groups and youth, will involve the following activities: updating the ETIs for admission to VTCs to include vulnerable groups; adapting VTCs' facilities for greater inclusion and for introducing innovative and outreach approaches (Modular, Multipoint, CBT, Open and Distance learning, E-Learning, etc.); training courses for different occupational levels; developing policies, strategies and guidelines for youth engagement in TVET programmes.

Output 2: Relevance and responsiveness of TVET programmes to labour market needs will require labour market studies and projections to be undertaken. Capacity of UNRWA staff in this area will need to be built. It will also require the strengthening of linkages /networking/partnership with the labour market and related bodies and institutions. Guidelines and criteria for upgrading workshops, laboratories and infrastructure will be produced. Competency Based Training (CBT) approach will be extended across UNRWA Fields of operation and support will be given to the development of appropriate curriculum and assessment tools. Training and ongoing capacity development of VTC instructors will be carried out.

Output 3: Establishing a TVET Quality System will involve putting in place policies and strategies for a TVET Quality Management System, through establishing a Quality Assurance Framework, a TVET Qualification Framework and, including recognition and accreditation by host countries.

Output 4: The development of coherent strategies and guidelines for empowerment and sustainability of VTCs will be important. This will require review of current best practices (UNRWA and international), optimization of resources, including through labour market partnerships and income generation.

Output 5: The Placement and Career Guidance (PCG) system will be further developed through a review of current practices, in order to conceptualise what is required for a more effective UNRWA wide system. Strengthening links with local and regional labour markets will be important in this respect. An Agency-wide electronic system for identifying regional and national placement and job opportunities will be developed to support TVET trainees employment, life, communication and entrepreneurial skills. Tracking system of TVET `graduates' will be strengthened.

Cross cutting issues

For the UNRWA TVET programme, cross cutting issues of gender, youth, poverty reduction, empowerment of women, protection, disability, and environmental protection are fundamental. In these areas, the TVET programme will benefit from engagement with a range of partners. To promote respect for the environment, new relevant topics will be integrated into the TVET curricula and new courses on the use of renewable energy will be introduced at UNRWA VTCs. The provision of short courses for young refugee women and men who otherwise would not have received formal training, will be another way forward. TVET will focus on providing technical and professional courses to an increasing number of students, particularly those from vulnerable groups.

Partnerships

TVET reform will require supportive partnerships, most specifically with the private sector, for the design and development of courses which provide market relevant skills and knowledge. The purpose of the development of a linkage/liaison model is to ensure that the TVET system is increasingly able to respond directly, efficiently and effectively to the requirements of the labour market by providing high quality, relevantly skilled and competent technical and vocational graduates. With regards to women's empowerment, relationships with local NGOs focusing on this area will be key, especially those working with regard to the participation of women in the economy.

Links with host governments

In order to increase cooperation and experience exchange for capacity building, on-the-jobtraining for trainees, accreditation and monitoring and evaluation, good links have already been established, and will continue to be built on, with the relevant Ministries, UNESCO/UNEVOC, universities in all Fields and the private sector. Through the implementation of the reform programme UNRWA will strive to strengthen these links and to establish new ones.

Programme management

The overall management of the TVET programme will be under the TVET and Youth Unit, Department of Education in coordination with Field Offices and more specifically with the VTCs. The TVET and Youth Unit will work closely with the sub-unit of Placement Career Guidance and with other units in the Education Department, most specifically ICT, Education Planning and Management, and Research and Development.

Monitoring and Evaluation

The Monitoring and Evaluation of the TVET Programmes will be part of the overall Monitoring and Evaluation framework of the Education Reform Strategy. Its design will incorporate the principles of Total Quality Management (TQM), most specifically in the utilization of appropriate tools and techniques, the formulation of performance indicators and the actual implementation of activities for standards monitoring and evaluation.

Curriculum and Student Assessment

Overview

5.7.13. UNRWA schools follow the host curriculum of the four host ministries and therefore the focus of UNRWA work in the area of curriculum will be on producing appropriate and relevant enrichment and conceptual materials for teachers and students. Driven by a broad policy and unified curriculum standards, this programme will work to support the development of children's understanding of the core subject areas: Arabic language, English language, Maths, and Science. It will also support cross-cutting values and skills development, most specifically by the teaching and promotion of Human Rights and life skills, and increasing students' understanding of tolerance through the teaching of non-violent communication and conflict resolution.

Outcome:	Curricula to support holistic approach to learning and personal development strengthened
Outputs	
Outputs 1	Policy and standards for curricula in place
Outputs 2	A systematic and holistic assessment approach in place
Outputs 3	A culture of human rights, conflict resolution and tolerance in place
Outputs 4	Students' life skills enhanced

Output 1: Analysis of current text books, with regard to conceptual sequencing, gender sensitivity, and overall neutrality, will be required in order to provide the necessary support to Fields in producing appropriate relevant materials. International expertise and collaboration with cost countries will support Agency-wide Task Forces and Working Groups in establishing Analysis Frameworks. To enable the evaluation of curricula and the application of standards, capacity of teachers will be built through training workshops and international expertise. Similarly, curriculum frameworks and teacher guidelines will be developed.

Output 2: A systematic approach for student assessment including the nature, frequency and function of assessment will be developed. A strategy will be put in place for administering a range of tests (for example MLA, TIMSS, PISA) in the core subjects to monitor and evaluate students' attainment and progress. Planning, preparing, implementing and administering unified tests will require full collaboration and coordination between the Fields and HQ (A). The capacity of teachers in student formative assessment will be developed through the UNRWA wide School Based Teacher Development Programme.

Output 3: The current Human Rights, Conflict Resolution and Tolerance (HRCRT) project, supported by the U.S., seeks to develop a Human Rights Policy and Strategy for UNRWA. A number of consultative forums will be held with education staff and the wider community in the Fields. Partnership with NGOs and other stakeholders engaged in Human Rights education will be a crucial part of addressing this key area of children's learning. Following the development of the policy and strategy, appropriate Human Rights enrichment materials will be produced. Systematic analysis of current curricula with regards to HRCRT concepts will be undertaken through the expertise developed and systems established under Output 1.

Output 4: To achieve this Output there will be an analysis of current curricula in order to identify opportunities for addressing the development of life skills through enrichment materials. A range of tools to assess the impact of these enrichment materials on students' behaviour will subsequently need to be developed.

Cross cutting issues

Cross cutting issues are particular pertinent for curriculum development. Issues of gender equity, inclusiveness, human rights and values need to be reflected in all curriculum material for children. Life skills, such as communication, empathy and respect, need to be addressed both explicitly and implicitly in curriculum and teacher support material.

Partnerships

In relation to the development of curriculum enrichment materials, UNRWA has established good partnerships across the five Fields, most specifically with The British Council and the American Centre. It is also intended to draw upon the expertise of the UNESCO International

Bureau of Education (IBE), global Centre for curriculum development. With regard to Human Rights education, the HRCRT project currently being implemented seeks to establish strong relationships with those working in the area of education and human rights across the region.

Links with host governments

As UNRWA follows the curriculum of the host governments this is an area where it is crucial that there is collaboration with the Ministries of Education, most specifically the Curricular Divisions, particularly with regard to curriculum changes and development, and subsequent teacher training requirements. Similarly with regard to national and unified tests UNRWA will need to continue to work closely with hosts.

Programme management

The Curriculum Unit, as with other Units in the HQ, is in place to support quality education across UNRWA Fields. It works, in tandem with the Fields, especially with EDCs, Ministries of Education, school supervisors and school principals. It will also be necessary to work closely with the Teacher Development and School Empowerment Unit and the PACICT unit, particularly when dealing with strategies for the use of e-learning, computerised lessons, distance-learning and on-line testing.

The Research Unit will also play a significant role through conducting research studies with regard to students' test results. For example, research studies can be conducted on the impact of newly introduced curricula, or on issues pertaining to students' attainment such as dropouts, over-crowded classes, double-shifts and teaching strategies.

Monitoring and Evaluation

This will be through implementation of a Monitoring and Evaluation plan developed for the overall Education Reform Programme. There will need to be Monitoring and Evaluation mechanisms in place to address this specific reform focus area. Links with the host governments and their monitoring and evaluation systems will be paramount.

Research, Development and EMIS

Overview

5.7.14. In terms of efficiency, UNRWA's education system is comparable to host government education systems—more efficient in some areas and less efficient in others. However, there is a great need for the timely, systematic collection and analysis of data to measure educational efficiency, effectiveness and equity across the five fields. Education policy decisions, within an evolving and resource constrained environment, need to be evidenced-based, acknowledge alternatives and be strongly articulated. In this respect, the Education Reform places great emphasis on research and development and an agency wide Educational Management Information System (EMIS).

Outcome:	Evidence-based policy making and informed decision-making at all levels in place
Outputs	
Outputs 1	Research and Development informs educational policy and planning
Outputs 2	Effective Education Management Information System (EMIS) in place
Outputs 3	Online library and communications system in place

Output 1: A Research and Development Strategy will be produced with external expertise engaging HQ, the Fields, other programmes and external partners. The capacity of education staff will be built, to initiate, undertake and validate research. Structures, such as research focal points or research committees, will be established across the Agency. Opportunities to contribute to regional, international forum and publications will be encouraged. Internally, a biannual Research Conference will be considered.

Research Briefs, based on international, regional, national and UNRWA specific research, will be produced and disseminated to Fields.

Output 2: The development of a strengthened agency wide EMIS will be achieved through the EMIS Task Force, led by the PCSU with representation from all Fields and external partners as appropriate. The EMIS will include student, teacher and management modules. All data will be gender disaggregated and a gender gap analysis will inform policy making and strategy development. Common Indicators based on universally accepted definitions will be developed.

Overall specifications and selection of EMIS software will be undertaken and both EMIS system and content will be piloted.

Output 3: An online information and library system is seen as an essential way of providing teachers and other educators with access to the latest research, relevant teaching and learning materials and a community of practice. Drawing on external expertise, a coherent proposal for establishing an online library will be developed. This will include a strategy for partnership and cooperation with national, regional and international associations.

Cross cutting issues

Research and Development will focus on conditions for achieving access to quality education for all, such as access for vulnerable groups, mainstreaming gender and protection issues, youth, sustainability and human rights.

Partnerships

The development and management of an online library and communication system will be supported through partnerships and links with international and national organizations such as UNESCO, UNEVOC, World Bank and UNICEF. Similarly, when such agencies are undertaking global, regional or thematic studies on issues such as refugee education, UNRWA will actively engage with them. When UNRWA undertakes research, or research capacity development exercises, it will seek to involve local, regional and global partners as much as is feasible.

Links with host government

At host country level there is a need for EMIS partnerships in order to ensure that UNRWA educational institutions are included in any national studies. Opportunity for greater cooperation with the host country governments, particularly the Ministries of Education and Higher Education, Statistics Departments, and with institutions and academia, will be sought.

Programme management

The overall management of this programme will be under the Research and Development Unit, but in coordination with Field offices and relevant Units in the Education Department.

Monitoring and Evaluation

This will be through implementation of a Monitoring and Evaluation plan developed for the overall Education Reform Programme. There will be a need for Monitoring and Evaluation mechanisms to address this specific reform focus area.

Governance

Overview

5.7.15. Good governance is crucial for successful reform and an enabler for effective programme management. An efficient governance structure is one that ensures policy is coherent, and decisions across multiple domains and levels are coordinated, minimise duplication, cost, and confusion and ensure decisions are made in a timely manner.

Outcome:	Effective educational governance system at all levels in place
Outputs	
Outputs 1	Standardised procedures for formulating, implementing and monitoring ETIs established
Outputs 2	Management for effective decision making at all levels enhanced
Outputs 3	Transparent and accountable educational governance system in place

Output 1: This Output is aimed at reinforcing and enhancing the effectiveness of programme management and delivery. Education governance structures will be in line with UNRWA overarching frameworks, and in cognisance with the human and financial resource capacity. Standardization of the procedures for the constant review, update, development and monitoring and evaluation of the ETIs - with the full engagement of all stakeholders - will be undertaken.

Output 2: An open and inclusive system, with clear mechanisms for communicating with all partners is crucial. The current lack of awareness amongst some stakeholders about the functions of various entities within the education programme will be addressed through awareness raising activities. Stakeholders will be involved in all aspects of developing, implementing, monitoring and evaluating an effective education governance system.

Output 3: Transparency frameworks allow for the open exchange of information among the different levels of the governance system. Such a system is more likely to encourage a larger community and stakeholder engagement and lead to improved support to schools. The UNRWA Code of Ethics will be endorsed, implemented and monitored. UNRWA will also strive to ensure a strong accountability framework with clear lines of authority, where the source of decisions is known, disciplinary mechanisms are in place, roles are clear and staff have incentives for helping to achieve the organisation's goals. Decentralisation has left some lines of accountability unclear in the current system and this will need to be addressed.

Cross cutting issues

Governance frameworks must acknowledge issues relating to equity of provision, either with regard to gender and vulnerable groups. They must similarly adhere to human rights principles.

Partnerships

Governance frameworks for education must be developed in line with broader UNRWA and UN frameworks. Expertise to support this area needs to be identified to ensure the successful development and implementation of a cohesive system of educational governance.

Links with host governments

Links should be made with host government governance frameworks as appropriate.

Programme management

UNRWA Education governance structure is complex, encompassing many organisational entities: schools; Areas; Fields; host countries and donor agencies and stakeholders. The governance structure is multidimensional, characterised by bodies/Units that have overlapping responsibilities across executive, legislative, and judicial jurisdictions. Governance will thus be managed by the Administration and Governance Unit at HQ, but there will be a need to work with the other Units of the HQ, and within the framework of the Agency's governance structures.

Monitoring and Evaluation

This will be through the implementation of a Monitoring and Evaluation plan developed for the overall Education Reform Programme. There will be a need for Monitoring and Evaluation mechanisms to address this specific reform focus area.

<u>Strategic Planning, Management and Projects</u>

Overview

5.7.16. UNRWA Education Department HQ will play a key role in overall planning and management of the Education Programme. This will include ensuring UNRWA-wide monitoring and reporting is undertaken regularly. The Unit will work with the Research, Development and EMIS Unit in sourcing data, analysing and populating Agency-wide strategic planning frameworks such as the MTS, Biennium Plans and those pertaining to donors.

Outcome:	Education programme planning and management strengthened
Outputs	
Outputs 1	Cohesive education planning processes in place
Outputs 2	Monitoring, reporting and evaluation system reinforced
Outputs 3	Agency-wide education projects effectively supported and managed

Output 1: Common planning processes, such as the HIP and FIPs, will be strengthened and effective operational structures will be established. Central to this will be adoption of Common Education Indicators based on global standards. Minimum norms and standards to support class formation, staffing ratios and field level operations will be developed, in full discussion with all Fields. Schedule of internal and external planning requirements will also be developed and adhered to.

Output 2: A Monitoring and Evaluation framework for the Education Reform Strategy will be the responsibility of this Unit. This will include appropriate databases and other measurement mechanisms. Periodic reviews will be undertaken to feed into ongoing planning of Reform implementation.

Output 3: Project management capacities and skills in the Department need to be strengthened, and a process for overseeing the management of Education projects will be established. All education project proposals and preliminary designs will be reviewed in light of Field needs, programme policies and Agency standards. The PCSU Project Management Manual will be mainstreamed.

Cross cutting issues

The responsibility for ensuring cross cutting issues are addressed, specifically gender equity, both directly and indirectly in the Education Reform, lies with HQ's Strategic Planning Unit. The Unit will ensure that UNRWA Education Gender Mainstreaming Strategy is taken into account in all processes. For the next Biennium, support will be provided to determine interventions to address the drop out for boys and girls and the gender stereotypes in the curricula. Furthermore, through its `project arm', specific areas of Human Rights will be actively addressed.

Partnerships

This Unit will work closely with Fields, other departments and the PCSU to ensure that strategic planning, project and reporting are in line with, and complementary to, other UNRWA programmes, practices and policies. Similarly it will be important to establish and maintain strong links with UNESCO, UNDP, UNICEF and with project and programme funders—again in line with UNRWA overall planning strategies.

Links with host governments

In the strategic planning and management of the education programme, relationships with host governments will be important. This will be towards greater collaboration and statistical comparison—for example in relation to student drop out rate, completion and achievement.

Programme management

The overall management of this programme will be under the Strategic Planning, Education Planning and Management and Projects Unit, Department of Education in coordination with Field Offices.

Monitoring and Evaluation

The responsibility for the monitoring and evaluation of the implementation of the Reform Strategy will rest with the Strategic Planning, Management and Projects Unit of Education, HQ, working hand in hand with PCSU and Fields. An overall Monitoring and Evaluation strategy will be developed to this effect.

Partnerships, Communication and ICTs

Overview

5.7.17. Although the Agency has achieved much in this area there is still a need to increase UNRWA's visibility and improve communication with both internal and external stakeholders. An UNRWA-wide partnership policy is currently being developed. The use of ICT at all educational levels is also emphasised to strengthen the implementation and impact of the Education Reform.

Outcome:	Partnerships, communication and use of educational ICTs strengthened
Outputs	
Outputs 1	Appropriate opportunities for partnership and collaborative links identified
Outputs 2	Capacity of education staff for effective communication developed
Outputs 3	Appropriate education ICT tools supported

Output 1: An Education Partnership strategy, aligned with the Agency overall strategy will be developed. Working with the UNRWA Partnership Unit, a situation analysis of current education partnerships and future opportunities will be undertaken. Mechanisms facilitating identification, communication and ongoing collaboration with partners through ICT will be developed.

Output 2: This Output will involve a situational analysis of capacity development needs in communication. Regular collaboration with the UNRWA Public Information Office (PIO), including specific training, feedback and appropriate support will be crucial. Hands-on training, with the support of UNESCO, in communicating with a range of audiences will be undertaken. Further capacity needs will be assessed and a strategy to strengthen oral and written communication developed and implemented. This will be in coordination with the Human Resources Staff Development Division.

Output 3: The development of an ICT in Education Strategy will involve a situational analysis and survey of the Education programme needs. This will relate to a number of functions: supporting the delivery of educational 'content' (distance and e-learning material); enabling establishment of communities of practices (Moodle); and putting in place 'small systems,' that is systems which, for example, will facilitate management of the MLA across the Fields, collaborative communication platforms such as `Base Camp' to support the TVET Task Force, and the management of the Scholarship programme. Capacity development will be required in all these areas.

Cross cutting issues

Partnership, Communication and ICT (PACICT) are areas that are relevant to all the other sections of the Education Department. For this reason, PACICT will maintain a very close relationship with other Units in order to best promote the work of HQ and the Field Offices. Communication will focus on topics including gender, youth, disability, the right to education, equitable access for vulnerable groups and education for Human Rights or disability.

Partnerships

This is one of the key foci of the Logframe of this programme area. At a strategic level, collaboration with the World Economic Forum, Education Partnership Forum, ICT companies (such as Cisco, Microsoft, Intel) and Media companies (such as Taalam TV) will be enhanced. The Education Department will also provide input, where appropriate, to the UN Cluster and

Working Group coordination mechanisms addressing communication of issues relevant to education.

Links with host government

ICT in education will coordinate fully with the host government Ministries of Education.

Programme management

The overall management of this programme will be under the Education HQ PACICT Unit, in coordination with all the other units, the Field offices and with external support as appropriate. The role of the Unit will be to strengthen the communication skills of the staff of the Department. Close collaboration with the office of the DE will be paramount in supporting the wider communication and advocacy of the education reform and general programme.

Monitoring and Evaluation

This will be through the implementation of a Monitoring and Evaluation plan developed for the overall Education Reform Programme. There will be a need for Monitoring and Evaluation mechanisms to address this specific reform focus area.

5.8. Structural changes

5.8.1. Implementation of the Reform Strategy will reflect the OD model, articulating clearly roles and responsibilities from the school to the Headquarters. Any successful transformational process requires front line staff to be actively engaged in the conceptualisation of the change and of the ensuing implementation process. In this respect, UNRWA faces particular challenges with the differing perceptions, needs and values of the staff and the complexity of the environment.

5.8.2. Classroom and school practices must change to ensure a more current and relevant approach to education. UNRWA's Education Reform Strategy seeks to bring strategic coherence to educational programme delivery, whilst recognising the contextualising factors necessary among the different fields of operation. This will be affected through the establishment of Agency-wide policy frameworks, standards and norms, as well as training materials for UNRWA cadres. Emphasis will be placed on training and supporting the professional cadres, most specifically the teachers, to enable them to engage the students in their classrooms in new and challenging ways.

5.8.3. Ultimately, the success of the education programme will depend on the balance of responsibility and skills held between centralised and decentralised functions. Decentralisation without carefully planned capacity building and an appropriate system of HQ support may lead to more problems than before, as decentralisation itself does not always lead to the outcomes expected (see Hurst in Lauglo and McLean 1986; and the work of Rondinlelli and Cheema for further details[4]).

---

[4] Chris Yates REF

5.8.4. Decentralisation in education does not always bring the expected benefits (e.g. greater efficiency and effectiveness through better decision making; more local involvement, commitment and ownership and more and more appropriate innovation). Paul Hurst posed the dilemma some 25 years ago in a seminal article entitled `Decentralisation: panacea or red herring?' The evidence suggests that the benefits expected of decentralisation may be forthcoming but they vary by context and situation. Decentralisation of education may be a positive move, but it all depends on what kind of decentralisation and how it is implemented (Yates, 2010)

5.8.5. It will be vital to build capacity systematically to support the decentralisation processes. Key to this will be an analysis of the current education support structures to ensure that the change in classroom practice will be effectively facilitated from the school to Headquarters. To this effect, an Agency template for professional support structures is being developed, and this will be adjusted in consideration of contextual factors in UNRWA's Fields of operation. Similarly, Education/HR Technical Instructions and/or norms of staffing and class formation exercises will be adjusted to reflect minimum structures and standards.

5.8.6. The Universalia Report suggests that `the move to a more decentralised structure would move the system away from providing direct services and more to providing strategic planning, oversight, and system level capacity building' (UO&M, p35). Supporting this, the Headquarters Education Department has been restructured. There are now eight Units; four Core Units focused on service delivery and four Support Units focused on delivering an enabling environment to facilitate evidence-based policy and informed decision making. See following diagram.

Diagram: *Education Department, HQ: Restructuring for Reform*

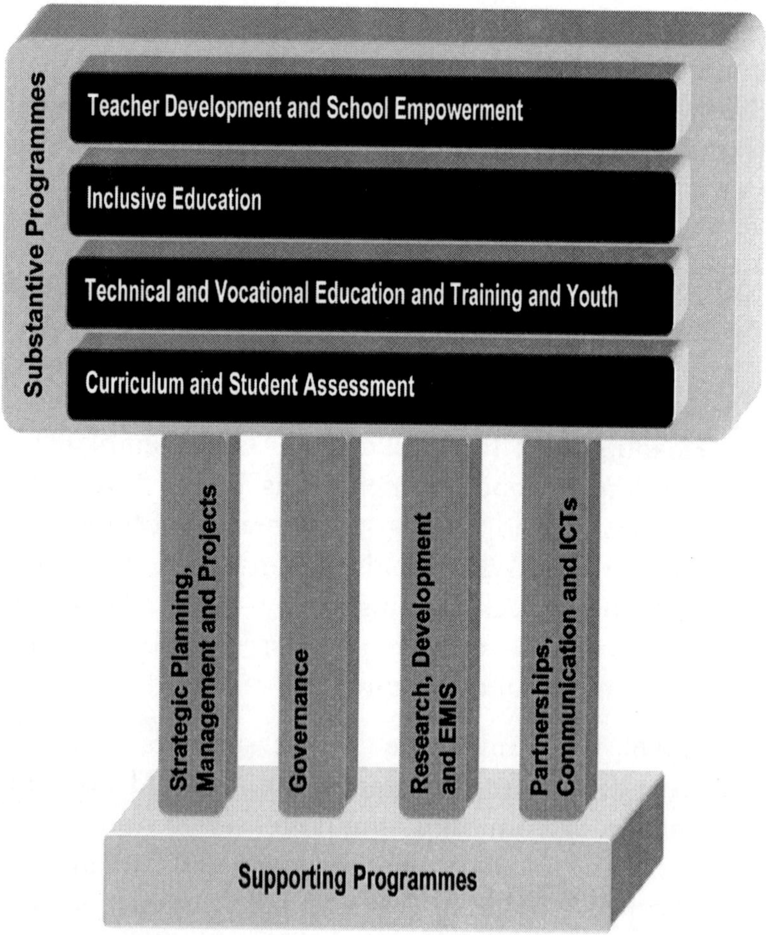

5.8.7. In the first phase of the Reform the Education Department, HQ will work with the Fields to develop policies, strategic systems and structures and training programmes for front line clients (Teachers, Headteachers and School Supervisors). Ultimately, once the systems and structures are in place, the Education Department will perform monitoring and evaluation, quality assurance and technical support functions. There may be a need to continue to provide in-service teacher education, through a more modern, diversified approach, using mixed mode and blended learning models.

Chapter 6

Implementation

6.1. Overview

6.1.1. In line with the UNRWA OD process, service delivery is the responsibility of the Fields but, reflecting the parameters established by UNRWA Education policies, standards and norms coordinated by Headquarters. Fields will ultimately determine the most appropriate model of implementation of any programme reform and will be fully engaged in all stages of development of the new policies, frameworks and tools.

6.1.2. The Universalia Review suggests that ED, HQ should work to establish the change environment and culture which supports and positively rewards innovation. The Reform Strategy thus seeks to do this through the design and implementation of an interrelated and holistic strategy, as exemplified by the eight reform programmatic areas. The Headquarters will lead the Reform process, ensuring engagement of Fields throughout, harnessing external expertise as appropriate and forging partnerships with a range of stakeholders.

6.1.3. Changing the way in which teachers interact with their learners, and what happens in the classroom and school as a whole, is central to the education reform. To achieve this major transformation, a Teacher Policy will be developed and implemented. This will address teacher recruitment, professional development and career progression. Coordination with the Human Resources Department will be paramount in this regard. Strong links with other UNRWA programmes and with specialists providing cross-cutting thematic support (such as gender, disability and protection) will be important and reflected in implementation planning.

6.1.4. The training of teachers will need to be comprehensively addressed through an Agency-wide approach. This will be through the production of high quality training programmes for teachers and schools to be systematically implemented by Field professional and administrative support cadres. HQ will lead on the development of the School Based Teacher Development (SBTD) materials, and will also determine parameters for the programmes delivery.

6.1.5. Funding for the Education Reform is being sought, most specifically through the `Sustaining Change' initiative. While funding is a key requirement to implement the Reform, there are existing opportunities for collaborative and innovative funding approaches. These could include consultancies shared between Fields and HQ, such as the current example between HQA Education and JFO on the development of implementation support material for the teacher training programme (for SBTD cadres like Head-teachers, Supervisors, Area Education Offices, EDC); seeking external funding by `projectising' dimensions of the Reform; `basket' funding across Fields, i.e. using project funds for one focus area, e.g. for SBTD course material (economy of scale); Field project funding to lead on one dimension of the Reform on behalf of the whole agency.

6.1.6. As highlighted earlier, successful transformational requires front line staff to be engaged in the change process. Commitment at all levels will therefore be essential to the Reform success—i.e. from the Executive Office to the school and communities. The effective delivery of a comprehensive, coherent and targeted Advocacy and Communication strategy can help to achieve this shared commitment.

6.1.7. The UNRWA Education Reform is comprised of substantive activities. The substantive activities proposed must be mainstreamed into current education programme delivery. Planning Guidance for the FIPs, provided by the Education Department will identify the Reform activities for each biennium.

6.2. Partnership

6.2.1. Partnership is of paramount importance for Agency reform. In education, there are existing, enduring partnership frameworks at global, regional, and national level. Addressing the Universalia observation that UNRWA partnerships were lacking, the Reform aims to strengthen the link between UNRWA and UNESCO at both strategic and operational levels. In addition, private sector engagement will be actively encouraged, particularly with regard to use of Information Communication Technology for teachers, students and TVET.

6.2.2. Nationally, host government partnerships are of significance first and foremost in their role as host to the Palestine refugees. Operationally, host systems are potentially alternative providers of education, recipients of UNRWA students in the secondary cycle and sources of teaching and support staff. As already noted, UNRWA schools adhere to the curriculum and some of the exams, of the host country. As a result, host education arrangements have an impact on the UNRWA education system both from an inputs and outputs perspective.

6.2.3. The Universalia Review notes that the host government arrangements are of central significance to UNRWA operations. It also suggests that `the significance of the host Government partnerships has not previously been articulated strategically by the ED'. It advocates that the value, implications and significance of the arrangements with the hosts need to be reviewed critically, and their future strategic significance assessed.

6.2.4. However, as Yates (2010) highlights, there are many ambiguities, tensions and contradictions in the Palestinian—host government education relations. For example, the curricula of host countries have to be followed as part of the agreement for residency (good citizenship/stable host states). Nevertheless, a key goal is to also foster an independent Palestinian identity and to preserve the Palestinian heritage, tradition and culture. As he suggests, any Reform Strategy must be seen to be giving these future nation building goals due regard (Yates, 2010).

6.2.5. Of strategic importance is alignment of the support provided by Development Partners, to host countries with that provided to UNRWA. For example, Development Partner support to a host country in areas such as, teacher development should include the UNRWA teaching cadres. To this effect UNRWA will work through its Advisory Commission, Host and Donors Meetings and in bilateral discussions with host countries, development partners, NGOs and the private sector, to further such an alignment.

6.3. Advocacy

6.3.1. To increase the local, national and international public visibility of the Education Reform, it will be necessary to collaborate with the UNRWA Public Information Office (PIO) and External Relations Division (ERD), to ensure alignment with UNRWA's global strategic advocacy messages. This collaboration will include coordination of advertising and advocacy campaigns, and a strengthening of relationships with potential donors and advocates.

Chapter 7

Monitoring and Evaluation

7.1. Overview

7.1.1. Quality monitoring and evaluation in the context of decentralization is crucial. This falls on the Agency at two levels: Fields and Headquarters. The Agency's role is to try to ensure equity through ongoing analysis of key indicators, adopting preventative measures and correcting disparities identified[5]. A more strategic view of the role of Monitoring and Evaluation (M&E) is required, and the M&E plan, operational structure and budget need to be clear.

7.1.2. The preliminary assessment of UNRWA's OD Programme highlights the need to establish indicators and associated baselines in the areas which the change process aims to impact. Specifically, indicators

---

[5] IIEP Newsletter Volume XXVII No 3, September-December 2009, p4-5

measuring cost and organisational effectiveness are referenced as necessary in order to track progress against plans. The Universalia Review also discusses the need for more robust mechanisms to facilitate a more holistic view of M&E. These mechanisms must be underpinned by strong and clear management information systems at the school and VTC level. While the Agency has made progress in the areas of data collection and information management, through the Results Based Monitoring system (RBM), there remains a clear need to systematically support Fields and Headquarters towards informed decision making, whether for evidenced-based policy, operational or planning considerations, with accurate and reliable information.

7.1.3. To this effect, an Agency-wide Education Management Information System (EMIS) is being developed. EMIS will allow educationalists and management to track progress over time. Furthermore, EMIS will be integrated into the RBM to facilitate the crossprogrammatic data collection and reporting for Field Implementation Plans.

7.2. Programme benefits

7.2.1. Economic Benefits: As detailed in Chapter 2, the region is facing a variety of economic challenges. One of the key benefits of the Education Reform will be the more effective use of existing resources, and maximising of comparative advantage and minimising costs. The Reform will also enable UNRWA's education programmes to become increasingly relevant to the economic environments within which they are situated, through the promotion of greater private sector involvement, the development of robust financial accountability systems and improved capacity development at all levels. The reform will also assist with the achievement of Education For All in the MENA region, which in turn will result in higher rates of economic and social return at both individual and societal levels.

7.2.2. Social Impact and Poverty Reduction: The Education Reform has the potential to deliver significant and direct social impact in the five UNRWA Fields. The Reform will work to develop understanding and build capacity in all Fields, to enable the education programmes to address and reduce social inequities. The reform has the potential to significantly increase access to education for Palestine refugee children, particularly for vulnerable groups, and to improve the quality of the education all Palestine refugee children receive. Developing capabilities and skills through the provision of higher quality education for more children is likely to prove to be one of the most effective methods of enhancing life chances, and thereby reducing poverty and social inequalities across the region.

7.2.3. Protection Impact: The Education Reform Strategy provides a unique opportunity to help safeguard and advance the rights of learners in UNRWA education installations. The Reform will ensure that teachers are adequately trained and supported to provide a protective environment for learners. It will help teachers and their support cadres to develop a greater understanding of provision of the safe learning environment, one that promotes the psychological and emotional well being of the learners. Ensuring the absence of violence in schools, in accordance with the relevant ETIs and UNRWA Protection Standards, will be a key to the overall Protection Impact.

7.2.4. Technical Impact: The potential of the Education Reform to dramatically increase the technical impact of the education programmes is great. Focused policy, strategic planning, and technical support can enhance the capacity to deliver a quality UNRWA education programme and contribute to the technical knowledge of host governments and ministries, and local and regional institutions, to more effectively address educational challenges. The Reform will enable UNRWA to engage with current pedagogies, methodologies, styles of learning and teaching, and forms of technology that will better provide its students with more zequitable, flexible and relevant learning and training opportunities.

Chapter 8

Reform Sustainability

8.1. Key factors

8.1.1. The purpose of the Education Reform process is to improve the quality of education services to the Palestine refugee community. Reform in the Education programme is a key pillar in the UNRWA Sustaining Change agenda. From 2007 to 2009 the Agency worked to reinvigorate the enabling environment to support the effectiveness of the service delivery to the Palestine refugees. With many of the outcomes of OD addressed, the Agency is now shifting the focus from organizational change to one of transformation change. Sustaining Change will comprehensively address the core programme areas in order to ensure services are more efficient, effective, sustainable and transformative. Sustaining Change will seek to put in place cohesive, quality systems and structures within coherent policies, strategies, frameworks and operational tools. For Education, the ultimate aim will be to substantively change classroom practices. Sustainability will depend on the following key factors:

1. The UNRWA Sustaining Change is **accepted, supported and endorsed** by all key stakeholders in all technical and financial aspects ;
2. A **well articulated** UNRWA Education Reform Strategy including its core investment programmes is aligned with the Sustaining Change;
3. **Pedagogic and organizational improvements are actively endorsed** by Headquarters and Field offices implementing the Education programme;
4. Direct service delivery education staff such as **teachers and support staff are engaged** in the **reform process** with clear roles and responsibilities;
5. The success and sustainability of the reform outputs will depend substantially on the **capacity and motivation of staff at all levels;**
6. **Supportive local community** will be crucial and here the programme's advocacy and communication strategy will play a key role;
7. **High quality, appropriate and feasible interventions** in the education programme reform (e.g. open and distance learning materials and implementation structures).

8.2. Recurring cost implications

8.2.1. The education reform process will harness, build upon and strengthen existing education programme system and structures at Headquarters and Field levels. There will be a need for an initial outlay of costs to cover the development of all eight dimensions of the Reform. This will include facilitating an Agency wide production of training materials, training templates, policies and frameworks. It should also include establishing the necessary ICT infrastructure for elements such as EMIS, and Online Library. With regard to recurrent costs, one main cost will be the sustained implementation of the Teacher Policy, which will professionalise the teaching and education support at all levels—i.e. through recruitment processes, career progression and ongoing professional development. Its implementation will however allow for more effective deployment of the current teaching and educational support staff.

8.2.2. The resultant improved classroom and school practices from the Teacher Policy implementation will also impact positively on the way in which resources, currently used to provide `remedial' training or for student repetition or disparate teacher training programmes, are more efficiently deployed. However, ultimately the teacher lies at the heart of a quality education system and as such, an ongoing investment in their professionalisation is crucial for the success of the Reform.

8.2.3. For ICT infrastructure a full scoping is currently being undertaken with regard to the ICT needs for the Agency as a whole. For education some dimensions, such as EMIS and the Library and to a lesser extent for teacher training (ability to play training DVDs), do require a level of ICT infrastructure. Funding will be sourced for establishment of a minimal ICT infrastructure to support the Reform and the establishment of modern educational delivery mechanisms. However, it is important to emphasise that the effective delivery of the Education Reform is not dependent on a sophisticated ICT infrastructure. Implementation programme Templates will be produced by HQ, in discussion with Fields, to guide the Fields as to how to most appropriately deliver the Reform within their own ICT context. The estimated budget does not, at this stage, include Field specific ICT needs, and the outcome of an Agency wide ICT scoping exercise is awaited. It is likely that Fields may require additional funding for the establishment of a minimal ICT infrastructure to support the Reform and put in place more up-to-date educational delivery mechanisms.

8.2.4. Overall successful implementation of an evidenced based, cohesive education reform across UNRWA should result in future more cost efficient and effective deployment of resources.

Chapter 9

Conclusion

9.1.1. Education is the foundation of human freedom, capital development and wellbeing. Over the last 60 years, UNRWA has provided education to millions of Palestine refugees from three generations. The need to revisit the vision of the UNRWA education programme to ensure it reflects the changing global, regional and national contexts has been widely acknowledged. Similarly, the needs of the Palestine refugees have evolved over time and the vision for education thus seeks to develop their full potential to be confident, innovative, questioning, thoughtful, tolerant, open-minded individuals, contributing positively to the development of their society and to the global community.

9.1.2. Quality Education is dependent on the holistic, coherent approach—it cannot rest with the implementation of one strand, such as teacher training, only. This is why the UNRWA Education Reform draws on the Universalia analysis of the whole education system in order to determine what needs to be done to improve the overall quality. To this effect the Reform comprises eight (8) key dimensions, all of which interact and interrelate with each other. For enhanced teacher performance, teachers undoubtedly need to be effectively trained, but they also need to be well selected, trained and motivated through extrinsic and intrinsic means. The Teacher Policy thus addresses issues of recruitment, career progression, performance evaluation and professional support structures.

9.1.3. Similarly the curriculum and the materials which teachers use to teach their students need to incorporate conceptual sequencing, and reflect key concepts, values and principles. The development of the Curriculum Frameworks and the Human Rights material, alongside the teacher training, will thus seek to ensure that curriculum materials support UNRWA students' learning and their personal development.

9.1.4. Quality education must be accessible for all UNRWA students and to this effect the importance of an Inclusive Education approach, supported by a Policy, tools and classroom strategies is important. UNRWA students must have routes for their ongoing development to enable them to realise their own potential, as well as to contribute to their society's development. The role of TVET in this regard is crucial and a well designed programme, which is responsive to existing and emerging market needs, both in terms of technical knowledge and personal, social skills and attitudes of the students, can do much to support individual Palestine students and their community, as well as contribute to the development of the national, regional and global community.

9.1.5. Underpinning all interventions towards an effective, quality, relevant and efficient education system is knowledge and understanding of challenges, opportunities and of programmatic impact. To this effect, the Education Reform Strategy places strong emphasis on building the capacity of the UNRWA education cadres to understand the implications of existing research in terms of their work in delivering the education programme. It also will provide structures and support for staff to identify where UNRWA specific research is required, have the capacity to undertake such research, and to be able to reflect findings into programmatic planning.

9.1.6. The interrelationship of these key dimensions towards the achievement of educational quality is thus fundamental to the rationale, design and implementation of the Reform. There is then a need for their alignment with overall Governance frameworks. The UNRWA Reform will ensure that a clear, coherent Education Governance Framework, with corresponding Education Technical Instructions (ETIs), is in place. This Framework will similarly align with broader Agency Frameworks and Policies.

9.1.7. In summary, the Reform is designed to establish a strong enabling environment, whereby schools and teachers receive appropriate and timely professional and administrative support, decisions are informed by drawing on both quantitative and qualitative data and research, and strong governance frameworks are in place and embodied in a comprehensive set of education policies and frameworks. This enabling environment will facilitate educationally, technically and economically meaningful progress towards the achievement of quality education for Palestine refugees. The Reform objectives are in line with the overall UNRWA Sustaining Change agenda, Medium Term Strategy and national, regional and global Education For All aspirations.

Annexes 1

Flexibility of Host Country TVET Systems

Flexibility of Technical and Vocational Education and Training (TVET) systems in selected MENA countries

Jordan

Jordan's education system is one of the region's most flexible, providing pathways between academic and vocational streams. Only those attending applied secondary schools (6% of students) are not provided the option of continuing education at the tertiary level.

Syria

Regulations limit the flexibility of the VET system. There are no options for re-entering the formal school system or for lifelong learning. One recent study referred to vocational education in Syria as a "second-best type of education with only tenuous links to more promising career streams."

West Bank and Gaza

15–20% of vocational education graduates make use of their option of pursuing tertiary education at community colleges. Those who have participated in vocational training at the secondary level, however, are denied this option due to the lack of theoretical content in the curriculum.

Lebanon

Lebanon's system has very limited flexibility. Attention must be given to enabling students to move between TVET and mainstream education.

Source: Adapted from Luinstra 2006 in World Bank 2008

Annexes 2

Key Donor Information by Country

Jordan

- Total aid to education (overall) in 2007 was $122 million. This is an increase from $29 million in 1999 (GMR 2010).
- Total aid to basic education in 2008 was $75 million, equating to $89 per child.
- The major education donors to Jordan (committed funds split over average of three years 2006-2008, DAC CRS 2010): USA $36 million per annum, EU Institutions $35 million per annum, Germany $15 million per annum (There is no record available of the split between primary/secondary and post-secondary spending in Jordan)

Lebanon

- Total aid to education (overall) in 2007 was $92 million. This is an increase from $48 million in 1999 (GMR 2010).
- In 2007, total aid to basic education was $75 million, equating to $89 per child. The major education donors to Lebanon (committed funds split over average of three years 2006-2008, DAC CRS 2010): France $51 million per year, Germany $20 million per year, USA $9 million per year.
- Lebanon is one of the main Mediterranean beneficiaries of EU assistance, and the EU is its largest donor (ETF 2010a). The World Bank is a major donor to the education sector.

Syria

- Total aid to education (overall) in 2007 was $70 million. This is an increase from $44 million in 1999 (GMR 2010).
- In 2007, total aid to basic education was $5 million, equating to $3 per child.
- The major education donors to Syria (committed funds split over average of three years 2006-2008, DAC CRS 2010): Germany $39 million per year; France $25 million per year; EU Institutions $11 million per year.

oPt

- Total aid to education (overall) in 2007 was $45 million. This is a decline from $62 million in 1999 (GMR 2010).
- In 2007, total aid to basic education was $38 million, equating to $81 per child.
- The major education donors to oPt (committed funds split over average of three years 2006-2008, DAC CRS 2010): United States $13 million per year, Germany $13 million per year, Norway $7 million per year, EU Institutions $6 million per year.

Annexes 3

Core Reform Programme Logframes

Teacher Development and School Empowerment

Intervention Logic	Indicators	Sources of verification	Assumptions
Outcome: **Professional, qualified and motivated teacher force and empowered schools in place.**	• Systems of profession development in place by end of 2012 • All teachers qualified by 2015 • All teachers professionally accredited by 2015	• UNRWA Education Annual Report; HR and EMIS information systems; Teacher Policy	Stable political and security environment in Host countries UNRWA management, staff, Host governments and development partners support reform plans Adequate funding for implementation of reform Capacity and competencies at all levels are sufficient to implement reform programme
Output 1: **Teacher policy and strategic framework implemented.**	• Policy is endorsed by end of 2011 • Policy is implemented from 2012		
Output 2: **Coherent teacher training & professional development structures in place.**	• School based model of teacher development in place by 2015 • Qualifications framework for Continuous Professional Development in place by end of 2013 • Career Pathing in place by end of 2014	• Framework for Continuous Professional Development; UNRWA Education Annual Report; HR and EMIS information systems	
Output3: **Effective management of teaching profession, and administrative systems in place.**	• Teacher Services Committee established by end of 2012 • EMIS Teacher Module in place by end of 2013 • PER system in place for educational cadres	• Semi-Annual Meeting Recommendation Summaries of the Teacher Services Committee; HR and EMIS reports; UNRWA Education Annual Report	
Output 4: **Status and working conditions of teachers enhanced.**	• Teacher Code of Conduct in place by end of 2013 • Advocacy strategy for the teaching profession in place by end of 2012 • Career path in place by end of 2014	• Teacher Code of Conduct; Advocacy Strategy	
Output 5: **A model of school empowerment developed and implemented.**	• School Quality Reviews implemented in all schools by end of 2015	• Fields reports. • HQ EMIS.	

Inclusive Education

<table>
<tr><th>Intervention logic</th><th>Indicators</th><th>Sources of verification</th><th>Assumptions</th></tr>
<tr><td>Outcome:
Equal access to quality education for all children regardless of gender, abilities, disabilities, impairments, health conditions and socio-economic status assured.</td><td>• Inclusive systems and practices in place by 2015;</td><td rowspan="6">• UNRWA Education Annual Report;
• EMIS reporting;
• Inclusive Education Policy;
• School Quality Review reports;
• Field Inclusive Education Implementation Strategy</td><td rowspan="6">Stable political and security environment in Host countries

UNRWA management, staff, Host governments and development partners support reform plans

Adequate funding for implementation of reform

Capacity and competencies at all levels are sufficient to implement reform programme</td></tr>
<tr><td>Output 1:
Inclusive Education Policy and framework in place.</td><td>• Inclusive Education Policy endorsed by 2011
• Field Inclusive Education Implementation Plan by 2012</td></tr>
<tr><td>Output 2:
Systems to identify and respond to diverse needs of children strengthened.</td><td>• Number of children identified using the Field IE Plan*
• Number of children identified supported through the Field IE Plan*</td></tr>
<tr><td>Output 3:
Gender equity enhanced.</td><td>• Gender Parity (elementary, preparatory) for drop-out;
• Gender Parity (elementary, preparatory) for achievement</td></tr>
<tr><td>Output 4:
Healthy school environment supported.</td><td>• Percentage of schools meeting healthy school criteria*.</td></tr>
<tr><td>Output 5:
Psycho-social needs of children identified and addressed.</td><td>• Support systems in each Field for students in place*</td></tr>
</table>

** Baseline to be established through implementation of the Reform*

TVET Youth

Intervention Logic	Indicators	Sources of verification	Assumptions
Outcome: **Relevant and quality Technical and Vocational Education and Training structure/programmes in place**	• Percentage of students employed appropriately; • Percentage of students with increased means of livelihood*	• UNRWA Education Annual Report; • EMIS reporting; • Education Technical Instruction on Income Generation	Stable political and security environment in Host countries UNRWA management, staff, Host governments and development partners support reform plans Adequate funding for implementation of reform Capacity and competencies at all levels are sufficient to implement reform programme
Output 1: **Access to TVET, particularly for vulnerable groups and youth enhanced.**	• Admission of vulnerable groups to VTCs is increased by 10% by end of 2015*		
Output 2: **Relevance and responsiveness of TVET programmes to labour market needs strengthened.**	• Review of TVET completed by end of 2011 • Market-based methodology in place for all TVET programmes by 2014		
Output 3: **TVET quality assurance system in place.**	• Pilot TVET quality system is introduced at VTCs within the next two years.		
Output 4: **Sustainability of VTCs supported**	• Income Generation ETI endorsed by end of 2011 • % of VTCs that are self-sustainable*		
Output 5: **Effective Placement and Career Guidance in place.**	• Placement and Career Guidance modules implemented in the Agency-wide EMIS		

** Baseline to be established through implementation of the Reform*

Curriculum and Student Assessment

Intervention logic	Indicators	Sources of verification	Assumptions
Outcome: **Curricula that supports holistic approach to learning and personal development strengthened.**	• Standards in place for Core subject curricula by 2013. • Unified tests undertaken biannually (2013 and 2015).	• UNRWA Education Annual Report; • EMIS reporting; • MLA Results Report; • RBM system Biennium Plan Reporting; • HRCRT Policy; • SBTD training materials; • Curriculum Frameworks	Stable political and security environment in Host countries UNRWA management, staff, Host governments and development partners support reform plans Adequate funding for implementation of reform Capacity and competencies at all levels are sufficient to implement reform programme
Output 1: **Policy and standards for curricula in place.**	• Standards in place for core subject curricula by 2013		
Output 2: **A systematic and holistic assessment approach in place.**	• Capacity of teachers in formative assessment developed in place by end of 2015;		
Output 3: **A culture of human rights, conflict resolution and tolerance in place.**	• HRCRT Policy in place by end of 2011; • UNRWA-wide system supporting the analysis of curricula with respect to neutrality and human rights in place by end of 2012		
Output 4: **Students' life skills enhanced.**	• School Based Teacher Development materials incorporate student life-skills by end of 2015.		

** Baseline to be established through implementation of the Reform*

Research, Development and EMIS

<table>
<tr><th>Intervention logic</th><th>Indicators</th><th>Sources of verification</th><th>Assumptions</th></tr>
<tr><td>Outcome:
Evidence based policy making and informed decision-making at all levels in place.</td><td>• EMIS generated data is used to plan and review Field Implementation Plans and UNRWA Education Annual Report</td><td rowspan="4">• UNRWA Education Annual Report;
• EMIS reporting;
• RBM system Biennium Plan Reporting;
• Research publications</td><td rowspan="4">Stable political and security environment in Host countries

UNRWA management, staff, Host governments and development partners support reform plans

Adequate funding for implementation of reform

Capacity and competencies at all levels are sufficient to implement reform programme</td></tr>
<tr><td>Output 1:
Research & Development informs educational policy and planning</td><td>• Research Strategy endorsed by end of 2011;
• % completion of planned research studies undertaken annually
• % completion of planned research briefs disseminated</td></tr>
<tr><td>Output 2:
Effective Education Management Information Services System in place.</td><td>• % of schools using the school-based Agency-wide EMIS to report and plan, with all modules in place by 2015.</td></tr>
<tr><td>Output 3:
Online library and communication system in place.</td><td>• % of UNRWA schools that have access and use productively the on-line library.</td></tr>
</table>

Governance

<table>
<tr><th>Intervention logic</th><th>Indicators</th><th>Sources of verification</th><th>Assumptions</th></tr>
<tr><td>Outcome
Effective educational governance system at all levels in place</td><td>• All of Educational Technical Instructions (ETIs) updated by 2015
• Degree of compliance with governance systems (i.e., ETIs)*</td><td rowspan="4">• UNRWA Education Annual Report;
• EMIS reporting;
• Policy & Procedure for Monitoring Governance Compliance
• UNRWA Accountability Framework</td><td rowspan="4">Stable political and security environment in Host countries

UNRWA management, staff, Host governments and development partners support reform plans

Adequate funding for implementation of reform

Capacity and competencies at all levels are sufficient to implement reform programme</td></tr>
<tr><td>Output 1:
Standardised procedures for formulating, implementing and monitoring ETIs established.</td><td>• Policies and procedures for monitoring governance established by end of 2012;
• % of ETIs reviewed and updated, annually</td></tr>
<tr><td>Output 2:
Management for effective decision making at all levels in place.</td><td>• Establish communication framework for effective stakeholder engagement</td></tr>
<tr><td>Output 3:
Transparent and accountable educational governance system in place.</td><td>• Education programme implementation of accountability and transparency framework in line with UNRWA Accountability Framework</td></tr>
</table>

** Baseline to be established through implementation of the Reform*

Strategic Planning, Management and Projects

<table>
<tr><th>Intervention logic</th><th>Indicators</th><th>Sources of verification</th><th>Assumptions</th></tr>
<tr><td>Outcome:
Education programme planning and management strengthened.</td><td>• Common education monitoring frameworks produced to monitor and evaluate education programme implementation</td><td rowspan="4">• UNRWA Education Annual Report;
• EMIS reporting;
• Handbook of Common Programme Monitoring for Biennium Plans (PCSU);
• Education planning guidance for biennium planning process</td><td rowspan="4">Stable political and security environment in Host countries

UNRWA management, staff, Host governments and development partners support reform plans

Adequate funding for implementation of reform

Capacity and competencies at all levels are sufficient to implement reform programme</td></tr>
<tr><td>Output 1:
Cohesive education planning process in place.</td><td>• Provision of Education Planning Guidance for biennium plans</td></tr>
<tr><td>Output 2:
Monitoring, reporting and evaluation system reinforced.</td><td>• Common education monitoring frameworks supported by indicator methodologies</td></tr>
<tr><td>Output 3:
Agency-wide education projects effectively supported and managed.</td><td>• % of compliance with external and internal reporting based on annual calendar of reporting*</td></tr>
</table>

* *Baseline to be established through implementation of the Reform*

Partnerships, Communication and ICTs

Intervention logic	Indicators	Sources of verification	Assumptions
Outcome: **Partnerships, communication and use of education ICTs strengthened**	• % of completed implementation of identified ICT tools by 2015*; • Partnership and Communication Strategy evaluated by 2015	• UNRWA Education Annual Report; • Partnership, Communication and ICT Strategy;	Stable political and security environment in Host countries
Output 1: **Appropriate opportunities for partnership and collaborative links identified**	• Partnership and Communication Strategy endorsed by end of 2012 • % of partnerships with identified stakeholders in Strategy established*.		UNRWA management, staff, Host governments and development partners support reform plans
Output 2: **Capacity of education staff for effective communication developed.**	• % of identified education staff trained on communication skills*		Adequate funding for implementation of reform
Output 3: **Appropriate education ICT tools supported.**	• # of ICT tools deployed Agency-wide • % of schools with ICT tool access*		Capacity and competencies at all levels are sufficient to implement reform programme

* *Baseline to be established through implementation of the Reform*

Abbreviations and Acronyms

BBC	British Broadcasting Corporation
CARE	CARE International
CBT	Competency Based Training
CIDA	Canadian International Development Agency
CEDAW	Committee for the Elimination of Discrimination Against Women
CFBT	Council for British Teachers
CIA	Central Information Agency
DFID	Department For International Development
DRR	Disaster Risk Reduction
EC	European Commission
EU	European Union
ECD	Early Childhood Development
EFA	Education for All

ERD	External Relations Division
ERfKE	Education Reform for the Knowledge Economy
ERS	Education Reform Strategy
ESF	Educational Science Faculties (West Bank)
ETF	European Training Foundation
FESA	(UNRWA) Faculties of Educational Sciences and Arts (Amman)
FIP	Field Implementation Plan
FTI	Fast Track Initiative
GDP	Gross Domestic Product
GMR	Global Monitoring Report
GNP	Gross National Product
HDG	Human Development Goals
HDI	Human Development Index
HIP	Headquarters Implementation Plan
HRCRT	Human Rights, Conflict Resolution and Tolerance
IAF	Islamic Action Front
IBE	(UNESCO) International Bureau of Education
ICT	Information Communication Technology
IIASA	International Institute for Applied Systems Analysis
ILO	International Labour Organisation
IMF	International Monetary Fund
INEE	International Network for Education in Emergencies
INGO	International Non Governmental Organisation

IOM	International Organisation for Migration
IRC	International Rescue Committee
JEI	Jordan Education Initiative
LPDC	Lebanese-Palestinian Dialogue Committee
MDG	Millennium Development Goal
M&E	Monitoring and Evaluation
MENA	Middle East North Africa
MLA	Monitoring Learning Achievement
MoE	Ministry of Education
MoEHE	Ministry of Education and Higher Education
MTS	Medium Term Strategy
NENA	Near East North Africa
NER	Net Enrolment Rate
NGO	Non Governmental Organisation
OD (P)	Organisational Development (Plan)
ODI	Overseas Development Institute
ODL	Open and Distance Learning
OECD	Organisation for Economic Cooperation and Development
oPt	occupied Palestinian territory
PA	Palestinian Authority
PACICT	Partnerships, Communication and ICTs
PCBS	Palestine Central Bureau for Statistics
PCG	Placement and Career Guidance
PCSU	Project Coordination Support Unit
PIO	Public Information Office
PISA	Programme for International Student Assessment

PRM	Bureau of Population, Refugees and Migration
QRTA	Queen Rania Teacher's Academy
RBM	Results Based Monitoring
R&DU	Research and Development Unit
RID	Reform Implementation Document
SBTD	School Based Teacher Development
SEN	Special Educational Needs
SPARE	Strategies, Policies, Accountability, Resources and Envelopes
TDSE	Teacher Development and School Empowerment
TIMSS	Trends in International Mathematics and Science Study
TVET	Technical and Vocational Education and Training
TQM	Total Quality Management
UN	United Nations
UNDP	United Nations Development Programme
UNESCO	United Nations Educational, Scientific and Cultural Organisation
UNHCR	United Nations High Commissioner for Refugees
UNICEF	United Nations
UNRWA	United Nations Relief and Works Agency
VTC	Vocational Training Centre

Bibliography

Al Abed, O. 2001. Palestinian Refugees in Jordan. Forced Migration Online, University of Oxford.
http://www.forcedmigration.org/guides/fmo025/fmo025.pdf (accessed 07.10.10).

Barrera et al. 2009. Education in a time of global economic crisis. Summary from members of the World Bank's Human Development Network.

BBC. 2005. The West Bank Barrier.
http://news.bbc.co.uk/1/hi/world/middle_east/3111159.stm (accessed 07.10.10).

British Council. 2010. Jordan Education Projects.
http://www.britishcouncil.org/jordan-societyeducation.
htm (accessed 14.10.10).

Care International. 2010. Where we work—Jordan.
http://www.careinternational.org.uk/where-we-work/jordan (accessed 20.10.10).

Chatelard, G. 2002. Jordan as a transit country: semi-protectionist immigration policies and their effects on Iraqi forced migrants.

Chiha, M. 2007. Briefing note on non-ID Palestinian refugees living in Lebanon. Lebanese-Palestinian Dialogue Committee and the Danish Refugee Council, Lebanon. Beirut.

Christian Aid. 2010. What we do in Lebanon.
http://www.christianaid.org.uk/whatwedo/middle-east/lebanon.aspx (accessed 18.10.10).

CIA. 2010. CIA World Fact Book.
https://www.cia.gov/library/publications/the-world-factbook/geos/sy.html (accessed 16.09.10).

The Commonwealth of Learning, 2010, Hilary Perraton, Teacher Education: The role of Open and Distance Learning

The Commonwealth of Learning and Routledge, 2003, Robinson B and Latchem C, Teacher Education Through Open and Distance Learning

Davies and McGregor., 2009. Social protection: responding to a global crisis. IDS Bulletin, Vol. 40, 5 pp 68-77.

Economist, The. 2010. Take it off: A secular-minded government rejects excessively religious dress in schools. July 15 2010. Damascus.
http://www.economist.com/node/16595099?story_id=16595099&CFID=146551530&CFTOKEN=29833327 (accessed 22.10.10)

El Khoury, M and Panizza, U. 2005. Social Mobility and Religion: Evidence from Lebanon. In: Research in the Social Scientific Study of Religion. Vol. 16, pp 133—161. Netherlands.

ETF. 2010a. Lebanon Country Information Note 2010. European Training Foundation, Turin.

ETF. 2010b. Syria Country Information Note 2010. European Training Foundation, Turin.

European Commission. 2010a. Commission Staff Working Document accompanying the Communication from the Commission to the European Parliament and the Council: Implementation of the European Neighbour Policy in 2009. Lebanon Progress Report. EC Brussels.

European Commission. 2010b. Commission Staff Working Document accompanying the Communication from the Commission to the European Parliament and the Council: Implementation of the European Neighbour Policy in 2009. Occupied Palestinian Territory Progress Report. EC Brussels.

FAFO. 2006. Iraqis in Jordan: Their Number and Characteristics.
http://www.unhcr.org/cgibin/texis/vtx/opendoc.pdf?tbl=SUBSITES&id=47626a232. (accessed 10.09.10).

Frelick, B. 2007. Iraqis denied right to asylum. In: Forced Migration Review, Special Issue June 2007. Oxford: QEH.

Fullan, M. 2007, The New Meaning of Educational Change (Fourth Edition), Teachers' College Press

Gavlak, D. 2010. Jordan boycott `damages election credibility'.
http://www.bbc.co.uk/news/world-middle-east-10919961 (accessed 21.10.10).

Gladwell, C. 2009a. Educational Planning in the conflict-affected Occupied Palestinian Territories: Why the National Strategy for Technical and Vocational Education and Training failed and lessons learned. Paper submitted as part of Master's degree in Education and International Development at the Institute of Education, University of London.

Gladwell, C. 2009b. An exploration of the Capability Approach in the context of refugee education programming: a Jordan case-study. Thesis submitted as part of Master's degree in Education and International Development at the Institute of Education, University of London.

Global Campaign for Education, 2010. Back to School? The worst places in the world to be a school child in 2010.

GMR. 2009. EFA Global Monitoring Report: overcoming inequality: why governance matters. UNESCO Publishing.

GMR. 2010a. EFA Global Monitoring Report: reaching the marginalised. UNESCO Publishing.

GMR. 2010b. Education is the key to lasting development.

http://www.unesco.org/fileadmin/MULTIMEDIA/HQ/ED/GMR/pdf/gmr2010/MDG2010_Facts_and_Figures_EN.pdf (accessed 21.10.10).

Hanushek et al. 2008. Education and economic growth: it's not just going to school but learning that matters. Education Next, Vol. 8, 2, pp 62-70.

Harmon, Oosterbeek, and Walker., 2003. The Returns to Education: Microeconomics. Journal of Economic

Surveys, Vol. 17, 2.

Hart, J and Lo Forte C. 2010. Protecting Palestinian children from political violence: the role of the international community. Forced Migration Policy Briefing 5: Oxford University Refugee Studies Centre.

IIASA 2008. Economic Growth in Developing Countries: Education Proves Key.
http://www.iiasa.ac.at/Admin/PUB/policy-briefs/pb03-web.pdf (accessed 19.10.10).

IMF. 2010. World Economic Outlook. April 2010.

INEE. 2010. UN General Assembly Adopts Resolution on Education in Emergencies.
http://www.ineesite.org/index.php/post/blog_UN_GA_adopts_resolution_on_EiE/ (accessed 20.10.10)

IOM. 2008. Assessment on Psycho-social Needs of Iraqis Displaced in Jordan and Lebanon. Amman and Beirut.

IRC. 2007a. Submission to Iraq Commission. London.

IRC. 2007b. Uprooted Iraqis: An urgent crisis. Washington DC.

IRC. 2008. Five Years Later, A Hidden Crisis: Report of the IRC Commission on Iraqi Refugees. Washington DC.

IRC. 2010. http://www.theirc.org/where/middle_east (accessed 20.10.10).

Islamic Relief. 2010. What we do in Palestine http://www.islamic-relief.org.uk/ Palestine.aspx (accessed 18/10/10).

Jordan Education Initiative. 2010. About Us. http://

www.jei.org.jo/#/1 (accessed 14.10.10)

Lebanese-Palestinian Dialogue Committee. 2010a. About LPDC.

http://www.lpdc.gov.lb/Sections/sTopics.aspx?Type=1&displang=en-us (accessed 07.10.10)

Lebanese-Palestinian Dialogue Committee. 2010b. Camp Improvement Initiative.

http://www.lpdc.gov.lb/Sections/sTopics.aspx?Type=4&displang=en-us (accessed 07.10.10)

Nicolai, S. 2007. Fragmented Foundations: Education and chronic crisis in the Occupied Palestinian Territory. Save the Children/IIEP.

ODI. 2008. Humanitarian Action in Iraq—Putting the pieces together. Humanitarian Policy Group Briefing 30. London.

OECD, 2006. The economics of knowledge: Why education is key for Europe's success. Lisbon Council Policy Brief.

OPT MoEHE. 1999. Technical and Vocational Education and Training in Palestine: A National Strategy. http://www.tvet-pal.org (accessed 25.10.10).

Oxfam. 2010a. What we do in Lebanon.

http://www.oxfam.org.uk/resources/countries/lebanon.html (accessed 18.10.10).

Oxfam. 2010b. Education, and the Beyond Access project.

http://www.oxfam.org.uk/resources/learning/education/index.html (accessed 20.10.10).

Psychosocial Assessment of Education in Gaza and Recommendations for Response; UNESCO;

September 2010.

Questscope. 2010. Education in Jordan. http://www.questscope.net/education (accessed 20.10.10)

QRTA. 2010. About Us. Queen Rania Teachers' Academy.
http://www.qrta.edu.jo/node/24 (accessed 21.10.10).

Riera, J. and Harper, A. 2007. Iraq: the search for solutions. In: Forced Migration Review Special Issue June 2007. Oxford: QEH.

Samhouri, H. 2006. Gaza Economic Predicament One Year After Disengagement: What went wrong? Crown Centre for Middle East Studies.

Save the Children. 2009. Life on the Edge: The struggle to survive and the impact of forced displacement in high risk areas of the Occupied Palestinian Territory. Research Report. Save the Children UK. London.

Save the Children. 2010a. The Future is Now: The Challenge of Education in Conflict Affected Fragile States. International Save the Children Alliance. London.

Save the Children. 2010b. Occupied Palestinian Territory Country Annual Plan 2010. Save the Children UK. London.

Save the Children. 2010c. Education—Quality matters. Policy Brief. Save the Children UK. London.

Save the Children. 2010d. Gaza Questions and Answers. Save the Children UK. London.

Save the Children and CfBT. 2010. A Literature Review of Education Financing in Conflict Affected Fragile States.

Sherwood, H. 2010. Netanyahu urges restraint as West Bank settlement building freeze is lifted. The Guardian, 26th September 2010.
http://news.bbc.co.uk/1/hi/world/middle_east/3111159.stm (accessed 07.10.10).

United Nations. 2000. The UN Millennium Development Goals
http://www.un.org/millenniumgoals/(accessed 8.10. 10).

United Nations. 2008. OPT Country Team Confidential Report to the CEDAW Committee.

UNDP. 2010. Human Development Report 2009—HDI rankings.
http://hdr.undp.org/en/statistics/(accessed 07.10.10)
http://www.unhcr.org/cgibin/texis/vtx/page?page=49e486566 (accessed 5.10.10).

UNESCO. 2010. Interview with Haif Bannayan, Chief Executive Officer for the Jordan Education Initiative. http://www.unesco.org/en/education/dynamic-content-single-view/news/interview_with_haif_bannayan_chief_executive_officer_of_the_jordan_education_initiative/back/9195/cHash/21adba25b9/ (accessed 22.10.10)

UNESCO, 2010. Psychosocial Assessment of Education in Gaza and Recommendations for Response;

UNHCR. 2009a. Country Operations Profile: Jordan.

UNHCR. 2010a. Iraqi refugees in Syria reluctant to return home permanently: survey.
http://www.unhcr.org/4caf376c6.html (accessed 21.10. 10)

UNHCR. 2010b. Syria Fact Sheet August 2010. http://www.unhcr.org/4c907abd9.html (accessed 21.10.10).

Universalia. 2010. Review and Forward-Looking Assessment of UNRWA Teacher Education.

UNRWA. 2009a. Lebanon Field Assessment.

UNWRA. 2009b. Gaza Field Assessment.

UNRWA. 2009c. West Bank Field Assessment.

UNRWA. 2009d. Syrian Arab Republic Field Assessment.

UNRWA. 2010a. Rhetoric and Reality—Human Rights and Palestine Refugees.
http://www.unrwa.org/etemplate.php?id=400 (accessed 07.10.10)

UNRWA. 2010b. Medium Terms Strategy. Amman.

UNRWA. 2010c. Draft policy and strategy for TVET. Amman.

UNRWA. 2010d. Draft special education background paper. Amman.

UNRWA2010e. The Handbook of Common Programme Monitoring for 2010-11 Biennium Plans. PCSU (Headquarters, Amman).

Women's Commission for Refugee Women and Children. 2007. Iraqi refugees in Jordan: Desperate and alone. New York.

World Bank. 2008a. Social Protection Enhancement Project: Hashemite Kingdom of Jordan. Project Appraisal Document. Washington DC.

World Bank. 2008b. The Road Not Travelled—Education Reform in the Middle East and Africa. Washington DC.

World Bank. 2010a. Lebanon Implementation, Completion and Results Report. Human Development Sector, MENA Region.

World Bank. 2010b. Education Reform for the Knowledge Economy II. Jordan Project Appraisal Document.

World Bank. 2010c. Lebanon Implementation and Results Report. Education Development Project.

World Bank Human Development Sector, MENA Region.

World Vision. 2010. Our work in Jordan, Lebanon and the oPt.

http://meero.worldvision.org/news_article.php?newsID=2116 (accessed 18.10.10)

Yates C, 2010, Taken from reports on missions and workshops towards UNRWA reform strategy development

Index